D1072477

"Working in heavy metal, Mr. Ginnever is lighter than air."
— Grace Glueck, *New York Times*, May 21, 1983

"In a world that prizes signature styles and instant recognition, Ginnever slows down and challenges the viewer's experience. He inculcates us with a nagging doubt, which becomes part of the pleasure of the work."
— John Yau, hyperallergic.com, Jan. 13, 2013

"The reduction of the vocabulary to its essential form is one of the factors in the existential dynamics of Ginnever's work. … These apparently geometric and minimal forms carry within them the entire memory of our civilization—our past, and our entrance to the future—and are not of an age, unless it is an imagined one: they are linked to the immemorial history of the space-time of our poetical thought. These are documents of vitalism in its pure state."
— Pierre Restany, 1987

"The few modern sculptors of importance, including Charles Ginnever, have provided their art with reasons for being that only it can demonstrate. Complex formal structures of striking coherence and energy, Ginnever's sculptures are something more. The foldings and unfolding of planar form mirror the work's effect of opening up unnoticed depths in the flow of mundane experience."
— Kenneth Baker, *San Francisco Chronicle*, 2000

"To sketch his achievement: he released sculpture from the right-angled—in other words, architectural—premises that have enclosed it since antiquity. Having freed sculptural form, he gave it the force of human gesture, at a monumental scale. Thus he has a connection to the heroic, gestural painters of the Abstract Expressionist generation, yet his forms are his own. Rather than recapitulate Abstract Expressionism in three-dimensions, he reinvented it on terms entirely his own. He found a future for the heroic gesture, and he is still doing it. A major achievement.

There is more to say, about the way Ginnever's works engage perceptions, turning the glance and the gaze into a gesture, but this is very subtle—not possible to summarize."
— Carter Ratcliff, *Art in America*

"Working in heavy metal, Mr. Ginnever is lighter than air."
— Grace Glueck, New York Times, May 21, 1983

"In a world that prizes signature styles and instant recognition, Ginnever slows down and challenges the viewer's experience. He inculcates us with a nagging doubt, which becomes part of the pleasure of the work."
— John Yau, hyperallergic.com, Jan. 13, 2013

"The reduction of the vocabulary to its essential form is one of the factors in the existential dynamics of Ginnever's work. ... These apparently geometric and minimal forms carry within them the entire memory of our civilization—our past, and our entrance to the future—and are not of an age, unless it is an imagined one: they are linked to the immemorial history of the space-time of our poetical thought. These are documents of vitalism in its pure state."
— Pierre Restany, 1987

"The few modern sculptors of importance, including Charles Ginnever, have provided their art with reasons for being that only it can demonstrate. Ginnever's Complex formal structures of striking coherence and energy, Ginnever's sculptures are something more. The foldings and unfolding of planar form mirror the work's effect of opening up unnoticed depths in the flow of mundane experience."
— Kenneth Baker, San Francisco Chronicle, 2000

"To sketch his achievement: he released sculpture from the right-angled—in other words, architectural—premises that have enclosed it since antiquity. Having freed sculptural form, he gave it the force of human gesture, at a monumental scale. Thus he has a connection to the heroic, gestural painters of the Abstract Expressionist generation, yet his forms are his own. Rather than recapitulate Abstract Expressionism in three-dimensions, he reinvented it on terms entirely his own. He found a future for the heroic gesture, and he is still doing it. A major achievement.
There is more to say, about the way Ginnever's works engage perceptions, turning the glance and the gaze into a gesture, but this is very subtle—not possible to summarize."
— Carter Ratcliff, Art in America

GINNEVER

GINNEVER

COMPLEXITIES
OF
MINIMALISM

CLARINDA CARNEGIE ART MUSEUM

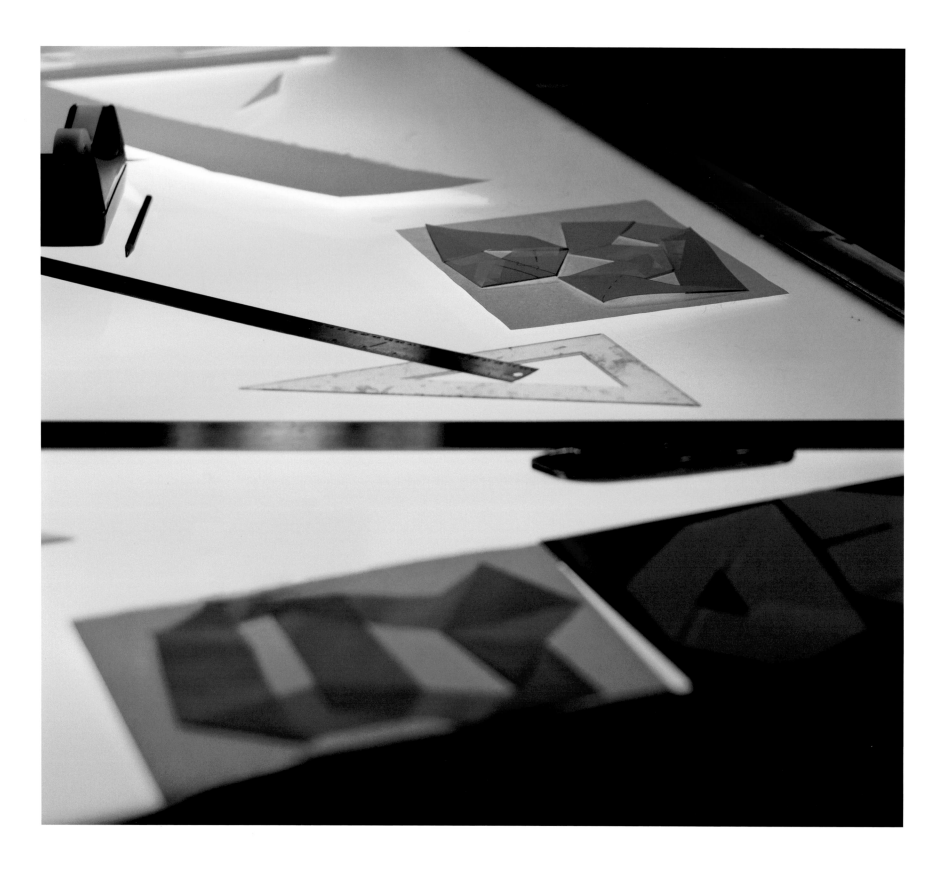

CONTENTS

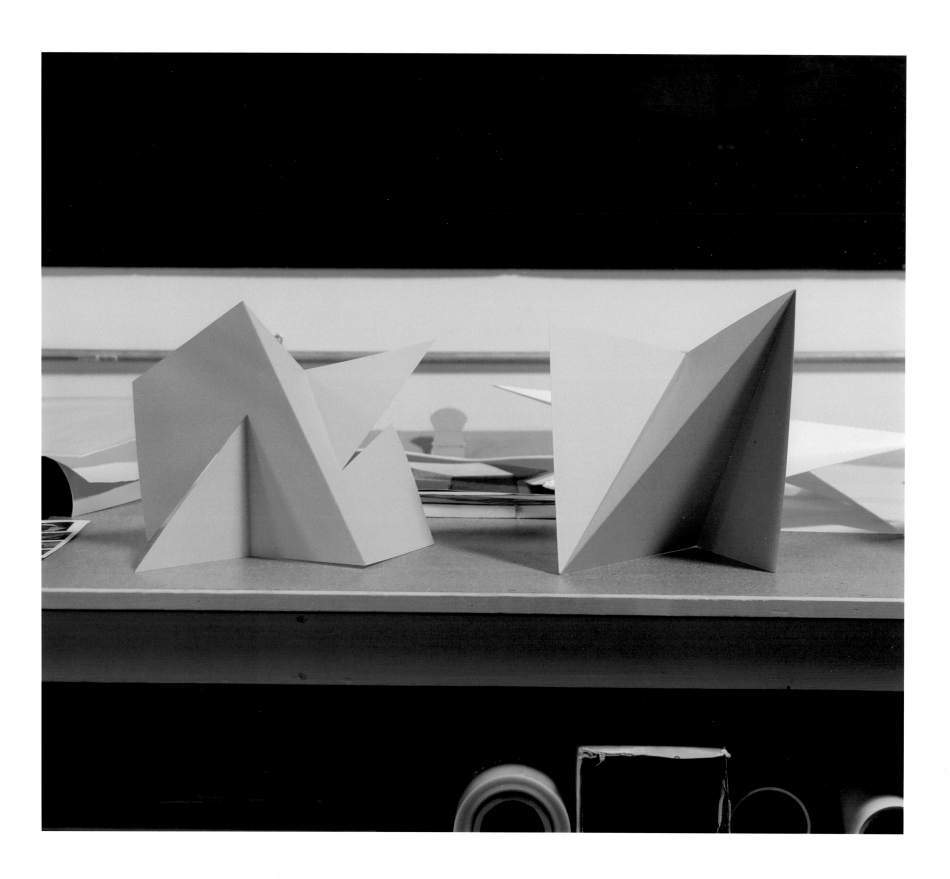

PREFACE

FOR MORE THAN FORTY YEARS, we have carried on a love affair with visual art.

When we first became interested in contemporary art, we were young and knew little about collecting. Fortunately, the Sheldon Museum of Art, almost in our back yard, had a new director, George Neubert, who had recently arrived from California. George was personally knowledgeable about the artistic talent on the west coast. He became both our teacher and mentor.

As our understanding of art grew, so did our passion for sculpture. We found ourselves drawn to the dynamic way in which three-dimensional art occupies space, perhaps because that is something the Midwest has in abundance.

Sculptures define their environments. They vary in scale from miniscule to monumental. Their surfaces range from highly textured to smooth. Their subject matter ranges from abstract minimalism to figurative realism. These encompassing characteristics intrigue us.

Almost without realizing it, we began to collect three-dimensional art. One by one they entered our collection. Women created many of the major

Zeus, 1975

sculptures: Niki de Saint Phalle, Magdalena Abakanowicz, Louise Bourgeois, Georgia O'Keeffe, Yayoi Kusama, Deborah Butterfield, and Beverly Pepper. Yet, we were equally enthusiastic about works by Dennis Oppenheim, Manuel Neri, Bernar Venet, Richard Long, Jun Kaneko, and Subodh Gupta, among others.

In recent years, Charles [Chuck] Ginnever's sculptures have become important to our collection. We have watched his career unfold over the decades, marveling at his ability to infuse each work with energy and complexity. Time after time, we have thought we fully understood a sculpture, only to realize later that we had barely scratched the surface. Ginnever's works offer a lifetime of discovery, which underlies our enormous pleasure in their inclusion in both our personal collection and the collection of the Clarinda Carnegie Art Museum.

During a recent trip to California, we visited an outdoor installation of Ginnever's sculptures and were told that they were going to be returned to the artist's farm in Vermont. We proposed having the large-scale sculptures make a stop in Lincoln, Nebraska, where our home is located. This "modest" proposal evolved into an ambitious project that would include nine works from California and almost two dozen from Vermont.

We could not be more pleased about our involvement with CCAM's exhibition *Charles [Chuck] Ginnever: Folded Forms*. We are thrilled that these sculptures will be exhibited on Clarinda's streets, as well as in locations in Lincoln, giving residents of both communities the opportunity to enjoy them daily.

We have thoroughly enjoyed getting to know Chuck, and appreciate his generosity and hard work during the planning of the exhibition. We also wish to thank Gayle Maxon-Edgerton, who has kept us informed about Ginnever's work and activities over the years. She and Anne Kohs & Associates have been immensely helpful in this project's realization.

Karen and Robert Duncan

OPPOSITE
Sculptures from the Karen and
Robert Duncan Collection
(See complete listing, pages 91–92)

Karen and Robert Duncan, 2017

xi

DIRECTOR'S FOREWORD

CHARLES [CHUCK] GINNEVER: FOLDED FORMS marks an exciting step forward for the Clarinda Carnegie Art Museum. It is our first exhibition of solely non-representational works, and we are particularly thrilled that the sculptures will be sited throughout our community of 5,000 people, as well as within the museum's walls.

Clarinda residents have been looking forward excitedly to this exhibition, which will not only offer an opportunity for people to enjoy the works every day, but, we believe, will build bridges with those who might have been a bit shy about visiting a formal museum.

With *Charles [Chuck] Ginnever: Folded Forms,* we will offer children's workshops, such as abstract paper folding and sculpture scavenger hunts. In the fall, students of all ages from the Southwest Iowa region will be bused to Clarinda for tours.

As always, we will engage our Junior Docents and a parallel organization for at-risk youth from a regional residential foster-care facility in their exploration of contemporary art and its place in the community. C-bloc, a group organized by CCAM and the Nodaway Valley Historical Museum, will look at Ginnever's art in the context of both art history and today's cultural climate.

Clarinda Carnegie Art Museum,
Clarinda, Iowa

xiii

We owe a debt of gratitude to our founders, Karen and Robert Duncan, who have enabled CCAM to offer related educational programming with every six-month exhibition. Needless to say, access to the quality exhibitions that we can organize from the Duncan Collection is an invaluable gift to visitors and regional residents alike. From the beginning, our exhibitions have consisted of top-quality art and have been thought-provoking and diverse.

CCAM's first exhibition opened on November 9, 2014, with *Our People, Our Place, Our Time,* which explored the American landscape and contemporary culture. Works ranged from Charles Guildner's photographic series regarding Nebraska Sandhills cattlemen, who continue to ranch with horses and cowboys, to Marc Babej's photo-essay focusing on how plastic surgery is used to achieve the American ideal of beauty.

Each subsequent exhibition has presented new opportunities for personal and community growth. *Crossing Borders, Crossing Boundaries* examined geographic, political, sexual, cultural, and psychological transits. *Beth Van Hoesen: Lyrical Line,* and its accompanying exhibition, *The Magical Art of Printmaking,* presented an in-depth look at linear forms in drawing and printmaking. *Manuel Neri: The Modernist Figure* took a universal view of human expression. The Neri exhibition involved another first for CCAM: the mutually beneficial opportunity to collaborate with Iowa State University Museums.

There is scant doubt that *Charles [Chuck] Ginnever: Folded Forms* will engage our community in exhilarating new ways. We are proud to show the works of a sculptor who has made an indelible mark on the history of contemporary American sculpture, and we are immensely appreciative of his willingness to share his work with us.

Trish Bergren
Director
Clarinda Carnegie Art Museum

ABOVE, LEFT/RIGHT
Interior views, Clarinda Carnegie Art Museum

BELOW, LEFT/RIGHT
Students in CCAM educational programs

INTRODUCTION

CHARLES [CHUCK] GINNEVER began his art education in the mid-1950s, a time of burgeoning ideas and creativity. New movements were tumbling across the art scene, pushing aside traditional ideas that were seen as old-fashioned.

As a student in the San Francisco Bay Area, then in France, Italy, and finally, Ithaca, New York, where he earned an MFA at Cornell, Ginnever had a front row seat to all that was happening.

He hungrily absorbed new ideas and paradigms: the muscularity of David Smith's steel sculptures, Stanley William Hayter's energized forms, Picasso's and Braque's interlocking planes, Rodin's elimination of the pedestal, Anthony Caro's color and constructivism, and Giacometti's manipulation of objects in space. Later, as a young artist in New York, he developed his ideas alongside his contemporaries who included John Chamberlain, Carl Andre, Mark di Suvero, and others, as they worked to take sculpture in new directions, organizing, compressing, and expanding space through their forms.

Throughout his career, Ginnever has retrieved nuggets of these early ideas, as he has weighed them, played with them, personalized them, and integrated them into his sculptural processes.

Ithaca, 1959

XVIII

The constructions of his nascent career, such as *Oxbow*, a 1958 totemic work made of recycled wood and steel (seen in this exhibition as a 1989 bronze), soon gave way to forms that shed any representational, narrative, symbolic, or allegorical reference.

From early on, Ginnever revealed a uniquely personal absorption with the interrelationship between his sculptures and those who would view them. He has worked through series as though they were branches on a tree, each one separate, but advancing this concept. It is this evolution that the exhibition *Charles [Chuck] Ginnever: Folded Forms* follows, culminating in his seminal *Origami Series*.

OPPOSITE
Oxbow (Cast 1/4), 1958;
Cast 1989 (two views)
Karen and Robert Duncan Collection

LEFT/RIGHT
Warp Series IV, 1963

Warp Series V, 1963

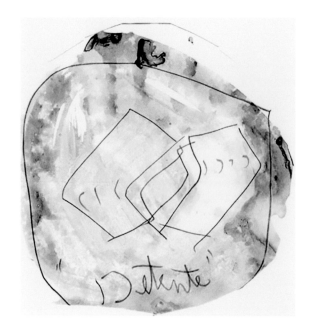

ABOVE, LEFT/RIGHT

Détente Drawing I, 1978

Détente Drawing II, 1978

Drawing of Four Sculptures, 1979

BELOW

Détente, 1974

Private Collection

In the 1970s, Ginnever began to create configurations of open-ended boxes that challenged viewers' conditioned notions of one-point perspective. Standing before one of these sculptures, a viewer becomes convinced that a move of a few feet will bring it into alignment, only to relocate and find yet another visual conundrum. Ginnever continued to explore these sculptural ideas into the mid-to-late 1980s. As one circles large-scale sculptures such as *High Rise*, 1984, and *Didymous*, 1987, the planes seem to transform into lines, visually diminishing heft, and adding buoyancy.

High Rise, 1984 (two views)

XXII

Didymous, 1987 (three views)
Runnymede Sculpture Farm, Woodside, CA

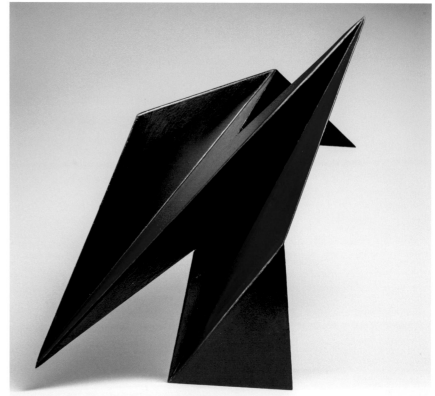

Ginnever also began working with some notable new concepts in the 1980s. He found that tilting sculptures forward gave them lightness and thrust. He expanded his context to infer movement, and, intentionally or not, suggested figurative references. From one angle, *Godard's Dream*, 1982, resembles a paper airplane; from another, it brings to mind a bird as it starts to take flight. *Luna Moth Walk I, II,* and *III,* 1982–85—three sculptures designed from a single template—suggest the graceful swooping and bowing movements of a Kabuki dancer.

The sense of spontaneity found in many of Ginnever's large works make them appear as though they have been bent and folded by a gigantic hand, and endures in his maquettes that are usually created after the construction of his larger sculptures. No sculptures characterize this freshness and spontaneity better than the series of works titled *Luna Moth Walk I, II,* and *III,* and the *Origami Series,* with elegant folds and colors that shift with the observer's viewpoint.

Godard's Dream (Maquette I), 1981 (two views)

OPPOSITE
Luna Moth Walk III, 1982; *Luna Moth Walk II,* 1985;
Luna Moth Walk I, 1982
Clarinda Carnegie Art Museum, Clarinda, IA

XXV

Most of us view objects from a single vantage point—ideally, from an easy frontal, eye-level view. Ginnever sees in a more complex, encompassing way. In an October 2017 interview, he described the first time he saw the landscape around Fresno, California, from the air in the early 1960s. He was shocked to find that its topography was echoed in his newest sculpture, which simulated the composition, organization of colors, and forms of the land below, just turned differently. Ginnever has continued to create topographical drawings, shifting his vantage point so that one must run through a mental file of possibilities to get one's bearings.

Another important influence is the landscape where Ginnever's farm is located, near Putney, Vermont, which he purchased in 1969. This is the environment where a majority of Ginnever's drawings and sculptures have been created, and where many of his finished sculptures are installed, nestled into the scenic hilly acreage that surrounds his home.

ABOVE, LEFT/RIGHT
Aerial Drawing Series No. 7, 1995

Aerial Drawing Series No. 11, 2000

BELOW, LEFT/RIGHT
Aerial Drawing Series No. 15, 2000

Aerial Drawing Series No. 12, 2000

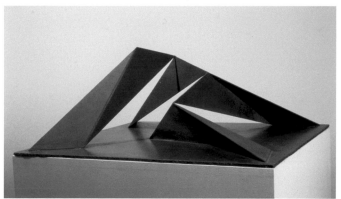

One might assume the lovely drawings of Ginnever's sculptures represent the preparatory phase of their creation. In fact, Ginnever depicts most of them after the fact. A number of his works actually began with a computer design program called Amiga, which allowed him to generate and manipulate compositions on his monitor, print them out, and then develop them as sculptural forms in space, cutting and folding Foamcore or matboard into models that would become metal sculptures. Ginnever becomes animated when he discusses this instant-by-instant, improvisational, yet calculated, decision-making process, clearly an aspect that has given his sculptures vitality and kept him engaged creatively.

Ginnever's creation of *Rashomon* in 1995 became a capstone to his life's work. Aesthetically valid from every angle, this sculptural form can also be turned on any of its fifteen sides.

LEFT
Atlantis Drawing V, 1978

RIGHT, ABOVE/BELOW
Atlantis, 1976
State University of New York, Buffalo

Atlantis (Maquette), 1976

xxviii

Rashomon was aptly named after the Akira Kurosawa film based on a twelfth-century Japanese story that relates the narratives of four witnesses to a rape and murder. The testimonies are so drastically different that one wonders if the witnesses have seen the same crimes.

When a set of Rashomon sculptures is displayed in all of the positions, it is almost impossible to hold any part of the form in one's memory long enough to apply it from one sculpture to the next. Each form appears unique.

Rashomon (15 units), 1999 (two views)
Karen and Robert Duncan Collection

XXX

"The main thing about my work, which has always had the same aspect, is that it changes radically as you move around it," Ginnever said. "But it's up to you. If you're not willing to use your feet and your eyes, you're only going to get a quick image, which will give you the idea you know the sculpture, when you don't. With *Rashomon*, those changes are astronomical."

Ginnever says that sculpture, like virtually all of his works, must be looked at comprehensively to grasp all it has to offer.

Those willing to allow their perceptions and assumptions to be challenged by Ginnever's innovative works can be rewarded with an enhanced ability to see more fully. The exhibition *Charles [Chuck] Ginnever: Folded Forms* is dedicated to that end.

Anne Pagel, Curator

OPPOSITE
Rashomon Etching – Nine Positions, 1994

Rashomon (3 Units), 1998
Private Collection

GINNEVER

The Problem is not how to finish a fold, but how to continue it, how to bring it to infinity. It is not only because the fold affects all materials that it thus becomes expressive matter, but especially because it determines and materializes Form. It produces a form of expression.
— Gilles Deleuze[1]

INFINITE FOLD: GINNEVER'S EXPRESSIVE GEOMETRY

OVER THE COURSE OF a long and venerable career, Chuck Ginnever has received considerable acclaim for his poetic, abstract works in steel and bronze. Despite the formidable weight and density of these sculptures made of angular sheets of metal, sometimes on an enormous scale, they appear to defy gravity. Ginnever employs a scrupulous and idiosyncratic geometry in each work, yet he follows no mathematical scheme or formula. The sculptures feel improvised and energized, as they sustain a sense of graceful comportment as well as rhythmic movement.

Nautilus, 1976, for instance, among Ginnever's well-known monumental public works in steel (in the collection of the Walker Art Center, Minneapolis), features a gently ascending slope of elongated triangles that radiate from a central spine, with open spaces between the joins, arranged on the ground in a subtle curve. Faceted in precise proportion, the units in *Nautilus* indeed resemble the pristine chambers of a nautilus shell. Ginnever's works of this period were often inspired by a visit to Stonehenge in 1974. His photos of the shadows cast by the monoliths revealed dramatic parallelograms that he later transposed into sculptural form. Despite the formidable scale of Ginnever's

Nautilus, 1976
Walker Art Center, Minneapolis, MN

1

2

public works such as *Nautilus*, they convey a rather delicate sensation of poise and balance.

The artist achieves a wide range of optical effects in each of his works by using dynamic sequences of bent and reconfigured geometric shapes. In particular, rectangular planes and triangular facets are primary elements of his sculptures. He frequently refers to these shapes as "folds." Distinct from a term like "bend," the fold implies an infinitely fluid process, an enfolding or unfolding action. In his unique visual language, Ginnever achieves a specific form of expression that corresponds in some way to philosopher Gilles Deleuze's study of the fold in Baroque art and architecture, whose reference to infinity implies a spiritual dimension.

A relationship between Ginnever's monumental aluminum sculpture *Godard's Dream*, 1982, for instance, and a classic Baroque sculpture, such as Bernini's *The Ecstasy of Saint Theresa* (the iconic 1647–52 sculptural group in white marble, in the Cornaro Chapel, Santa Maria della Vittoria in Rome) may not be obvious at first. The diagonal shapes in *Godard's Dream*, however, as they thrust skyward, clearly share the heavenly diagonal forces of Bernini's inspirational tableau.

OPPOSITE
1. *Godard's Dream*, 1982

LEFT/RIGHT
2-3. *Nike*, 1986 (two views)
APEC Sculpture Garden, PICC, Manila, Philippines

4. Gian Lorenzo Bernini (1598–1680)
L'Estasi di Santa Teresa (*The Ecstasy of St. Theresa*), 1647–52
Cornaro Chapel, Santa Maria della Vittoria, Rome

4

Ginnever's steel sculptures *Luna Moth Walk I, II & III*, 1982–85, convey an expressive geometry that also appears rather pliant and yielding. Despite the works' imposing scale and bulk, the creased and pleated forms conjure lilting dance steps, or the flittering movements of a moth, rather than the imperious and implacable presences one might expect. The zigzag compositions of the *Luna Moth Walk* series evoke a sense of the figure in motion, almost in Cubist terms. It is interesting to compare them today with recent abstracted figures made of fractured planes by Britain's Antony Gormley, and French artist Xavier Veilhan.

OPPOSITE
LEFT, ABOVE/BELOW
5. *Luna Moth Walk III*, 1982
Clarinda Carnegie Art Museum

6. *Luna Moth Walk I*, 1982
Clarinda Carnegie Art Museum

RIGHT
7. *Luna Moth Walk II*, 1985
Clarinda Carnegie Art Museum

8-9. *Luna Moth Walk I Maquette*, 1981 (two views)

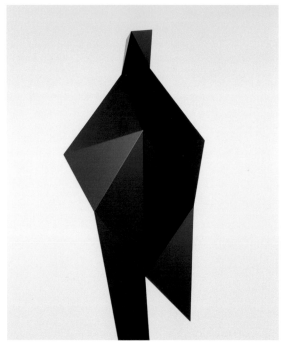

LEFT, ABOVE/BELOW
10. Antony Gormley (b. 1950)
Vessel, 2012

11. Xavier Veilhan (b. 1963)
Laurence, 2014
Collection Fundación AMMA

RIGHT, ABOVE/BELOW
12-13. *San Mateo Bridge*, 1978
City of San Mateo, California

Gormley's expansive steel constructions such as *Vessel*, 2012, for example, closely correspond to works by Ginnever, such as *San Mateo Bridge*, 1978, created decades earlier. Veilhan, who represented France at the 2017 Venice Biennale, is known for abstract and figurative works whose inherent geometry bears kinship to Ginnever's, especially in works such as his colorful geometric sculpture *Bop and Crazed*, 1980.

14. *San Mateo Bridge*, 1978
City of San Mateo, California

7

LEFT/RIGHT

15. *Bop and Crazed*, 1980

16. *Bop*, 1980

8

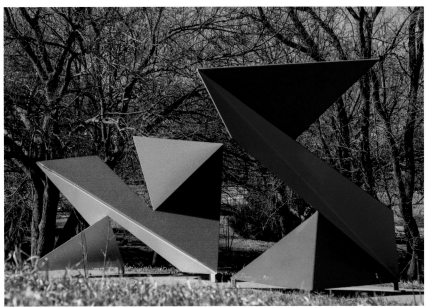

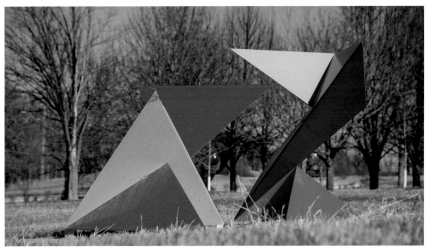

While rigorous in its conception, construction and installation, Ginnever's geometry is imaginative, instinctive, and full of surprises. "Mathematicians and scientists get it right away," he once told me.[2] His work encompasses perceptual games, and a consistent play of spatial relationships; but the process is never rote. Ginnever's is a personal geometry, gleefully unfettered from rules and theory. The geometry evolves as part of the artist's working method, and is not predetermined or planned according to a specific doctrine, or realized by following a formulaic system.

ABOVE, LEFT
17. *Crazed*, 1980

ABOVE, RIGHT/BELOW
18-20. *Bop and Crazed*, 1980

9

21-22. *Chicago Triangles*, 1979 (two views)
Iris & B. Gerald Cantor Center for Visual Arts,
Stanford University, Stanford, CA

Born in San Mateo, California, Ginnever recalls an incident in his early childhood that instigated a life-long fascination with spatial relationships, depth perception, and illusion. At about eighteen months old, his parents took him for a drive to the Pacific coast for a picnic. They parked in an area above the beach, and his father went ahead along a footpath toward the ocean. As he promptly disappeared from view, the confused and alarmed young Ginnever panicked and screamed until his mother took him to the edge of the cliff and pointed out his father, who was already near the water, a diminutive shape in the far distance.

"This was my first experience with the visual reality of illusion," Ginnever wrote in an autobiographical statement. "It has stayed with me and continues to influence what I do as an artist."

23-25. *No Place to Hide*, 1986 (three views)

12

Spatial phenomena and optical illusions are paramount in *Rashomon*, one of Ginnever's most lauded series of works. The title refers to the eponymous Akira Kurosawa film of 1950, based on the short stories 'Rashōmon' and 'In a Bamboo Grove' by Japanese author Ryūnosuke Akutagawa (1892–1927), which relates the same story told from the varied points of view of several characters. Ginnever's *Rashomon* features a modular construction that sustains multiple readings and endless possibilities for display. The shape, which the artist replicated and presented in a variety of configurations, may be regarded as a kind of Möbius strip made of narrow, twisted steel planes.

OPPOSITE
26. *Rashomon* (15 units), 1999
Karen and Robert Duncan Collection

27. *Rashomon Sculpture Study IV — Four Positions*, 1993

13

14

In 1993, Ginnever began to develop this concept of a singular sculptural form that would appear as an entirely new shape if replicated and displayed in different positions. The design seems to result from a mathematical formula, or an experiment with schematic serial imagery that could be related to Structuralism. And the artist embraces the notion of a minimal form, but without conforming to the Minimalist canon.[3] As always with Ginnever, the process that led to the form was intuitive and poetic. The endeavor preoccupied him for a number of years, manifested first in the 1994 tabletop bronzes, to large-scale steel sculptures, a series of etchings, and ending with the publication of a limited edition artists' book related to the theme in 2014. All the while he continued to create a number of other major large-scale sculptures and maquettes.

OPPOSITE
28. *Rashomon (Table with 11 Maquettes)*, 1994
Private Collection

29. *Rashomon* (Deluxe copy with maquette), 2014

With *Rashomon*, each of the identical forms can stand on any one of its fifteen sides to appear as a completely new and unique sculpture. Ginnever produced the form in a number of sizes, from intimate bronze, to large-scale outdoor works in steel, up to thirteen feet high. Furthering the metaphor of infinity that permeates much of Ginnever's work, *Rashomon* may be regarded as a "perpetual sculpture."[4] As a multi-unit installation, with the components positioned on the ground, a sculpture stand, or on a table top, depending on the scale, the sequence or continuum of unique compositions corresponds stylistically and thematically to the whole. By displaying *Rashomon*'s identical form in each of its fifteen varying positions, Ginnever challenges the viewer to make sense perceptually of the singularity of its geometry, even as each position appears to create an entirely new sculptural form.

Ginnever regards his entire *oeuvre* as a continuum. "You can take a look back to the early 1960s and you'll understand what I am doing now," he has remarked. "Chronology has nothing to do with what I do."

30. *Rashomon X*, 1994

OPPOSITE
31. *Rashomon* (15 units), 1999, installed at
San Jose Institute for Contemporary Art, 2012

16

17

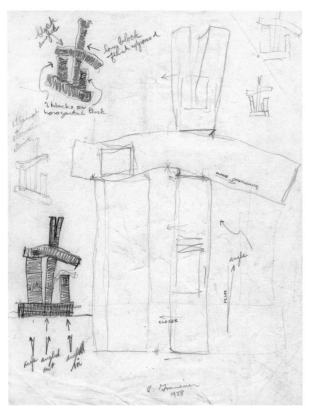

From 1953–55, Ginnever traveled in Europe for the first time. In Paris, he studied with the influential modernist figurative sculptor, Ossip Zadkine, and later with the printmaker known for sinuous abstract compositions, Stanley William Hayter. He met the American sculptor George Sugarman while in Paris, and they shared a deep appreciation for works by David Smith, who was one of the first contemporary sculptors to introduce color into his abstract works.

Ginnever enjoyed the Parisian café scene, where gathering places were still frequented by legendary artists like Giacometti, Brancusi, and Miró. Giacometti's pivotal Surrealist-period sculpture, *The Palace at 4am*, 1932, would have a particularly long-lasting impact on the young artist. Ginnever found, in this work's ambiguous spaces and construction of forms and proportions, that Giacometti had suggested a great deal more to be explored in terms of spatial relationships and three-dimensional iconography, ideas Ginnever has vigorously pursued in his own work.

Upon returning to the United States, Ginnever attended the California School of Fine Arts in San Francisco, and subsequently received an M.F.A. at Cornell University. While in San Francisco, he met Mark di Suvero at the studio of Manuel Neri. After he moved to New York City in 1960, Ginnever, along with

di Suvero, and another like-minded artist friend and colleague, John Chamberlain, embarked on an ambitious effort to create large-scale abstract sculptures that would bring Abstract Expressionism into a three-dimensional realm.

Ginnever was engaged for a period in the late 1950s with massive works using wooden railroad ties and steel. These attracted the attention of New York's Martha Jackson Gallery, where he first showed in 1960; subsequently, prominent dealers such as Allan Stone and Paula Cooper invited Ginnever to exhibit his work. In New York, he immersed himself in the avant-garde of the 1960s and early '70s, and formed bonds with other artists on the scene, including Ronald Bladen, Tom Doyle, Robert Smithson, Richard Serra, and Lawrence Weiner—fixtures at trendy New York clubs like Max's Kansas City.

Early on in his career, and far ahead of his time, he experimented with the interrelationship of performance, dance, and sculpture, emphasizing the body's movement in real time and space as an integral part of the entire sculptural experience. He produced and took part in "happenings" in upstate New York, artist carnivals for which he created "Sculpture Dances," performing with artists who included Allan Kaprow, Eva Hesse, and Tom Doyle, in wearable sculptures made of sticks and cloth.

OPPOSITE
ABOVE, LEFT/RIGHT
32. *Calligraphic Sculpture*, 1958

33. *Ithaca*, 1959

BELOW
34. *Calligraphic Sculpture, 1958 (Working Drawing No. 1)*, 1958

LEFT/RIGHT
35-36. Tom Doyle (left) and Charles Ginnever (right)
in Sculpture Dance, *Ergo Suits Carnival*, 1962

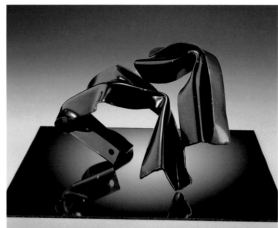

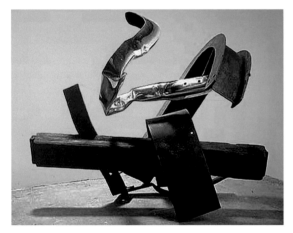
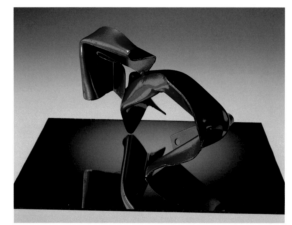

ABOVE/BELOW, LEFT/RIGHT
37-38. *Jezabel*, 1964 (two views)

39-40. *Steel Maquette with Mirror II*, 1963 (two views)
Private Collection

41-42. *Timebridge*, 1964 (two views)
Private Collection

After devoting some years to large-scale, found-object assemblage sculptures, Ginnever became increasingly focused on welded steel sculptures. Though self-taught as a welder, Ginnever became a welding instructor at New York's Pratt Institute in 1963. By the mid '60s, he was already renowned for large-scale, abstract, welded-steel sculptures featuring stark geometric shapes and meticulous construction.

A major breakthrough for Ginnever came in 1964, when he created *Dante's Rig*, a key piece in his *oeuvre*, which is on permanent outdoor display near his Vermont studio. More deliberately composed, indeed, more "designed" than all of his efforts to that date, *Dante's Rig* was inspired by a dream he had one night. In the dream, he was inside a California art gallery filled with a single, mysterious

abstract sculpture. Despite a gallerist's warning, he touched a part of the sculpture, which caused the entire piece to abruptly compress itself into a large tube.

In *Dante's Rig*, a steel support structure more than thirteen feet high holds two rows of parallelograms made of cut sheets of aluminum, "wings," suspended by steel wires attached to the steel armature. A sense of weightlessness enters Ginnever's work at this point. Less freeform and more meticulously constructed than anything Ginnever created before, this seminal piece harbors the unique geometry and a sense of playful comportment that would recur in practically all of the artist's subsequent sculptures. Although its modular construction suggests flexibility, all of the elements of this sculpture—unlike the one that appeared in the dream—are non-retractable and firmly secured in place.

43. *Dante's Rig*, 1964

21

ABOVE/BELOW
44. *Midas and Fog*, 1966
Private Collection

45. *3 + 1*, 1967
The Metropolitan Museum of Art, New York

Large, open boxlike forms appear suspended in space in his welded-steel works such as *Midas and Fog*, 1966; *3 + 1*, 1967, which was acquired by the Metropolitan Museum of Art; and Untitled, 1968, in the collection of the Hirshhorn Museum and Sculpture Garden—all part of his "Flat Illusion" series, in which flattened geometric forms appear to open and close as the viewer observes them from multiple points of view.

46. Untitled (Flat Illusion, for Joseph H. Hirshhorn II), 1968
Hirshhorn Museum and Sculpture Garden, Washington, DC

23

LEFT/RIGHT
47. *High Rise*, 1984, and *Medusa*, 1986, installed at Riverside Park, New York, October 2014

48. *High Rise*, 1984

24

From the mid-1960s on, Ginnever received numerous commissions for large-scale public works. By the end of the decade, he had established his reputation as one of the most inventive and progressive sculptors of his generation. A major 1975 commission from the University of Michigan resulted in a large-scale sculpture titled *Daedalus*, which is one of a group of sculptures identified by Ginnever as his "Spinal Series." With few exceptions, works in this series bear titles associated with Greek history and myth, including *Icarus, Atlantis, Nautilus, Olympus*, and *Koronos II*. The scale and grandeur of his public commissions increased exponentially over the years, leading to monumental sculptures like *High Rise*, 1984, and *Medusa*, 1986, the last work in the "Spinal Series." These two majestic steel constructions were installed in New York in 2014, in an impressive setting along the Hudson River at Manhattan's Riverside Park.

49. *Medusa*, 1986

Over the years, Ginnever's private and idiosyncratic geometry would seem to be reflected in the work of a younger generation of sculptors, such as Carol Bove and Vincent Fecteau, to name just two. The efforts of these artists address and reconsider issues of formalist abstraction, and explore an idiosyncratic visual language that has been part of Ginnever's sculptural vocabulary for decades. Ginnever would argue that his work is in no way formalist since it is wholly intuitive and follows no set rules, but the close connection between his pioneering works and the latest currents in abstract sculpture is quite clear.

There is an intensely engaging aspect to Ginnever's work, which makes it particularly suitable for public spaces. As viewers move through and around the monumental sculptures, perspectives shift and the sculptures' forms appear to change. What one initially perceives in the work, its rigid geometry and fixed perspective, suddenly appears mutable. Ginnever returns time and again to explore these perceptual challenges, producing works with shapes and lines that appear suspended in space. A work such as the tall, bronze *Azuma*, 1987, features triangular facets that seem to shift and stretch skyward, as if in a ritualistic dance. Abstract though it is, the image assumes vaguely anthropomorphic aspects as the viewer's viewpoint shifts.

50-51. *Dementia*, 1998 (two views)

OPPOSITE
52-53. *Azuma*, 1987 (two views)

27

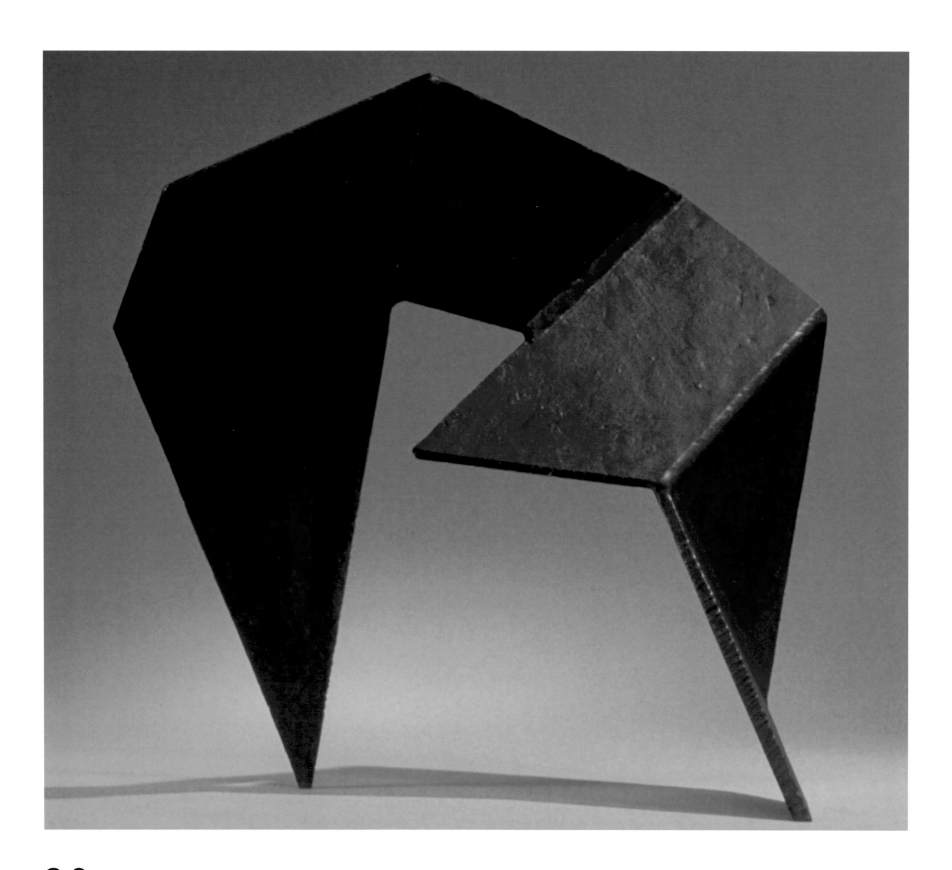

28

 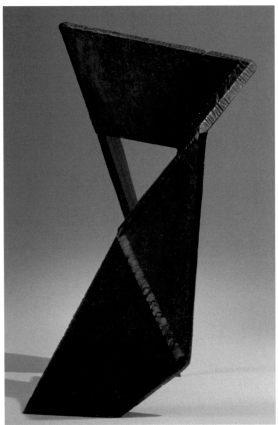 

Similarly, the austere and elegant works of the *Moonwalker* series, from the late 1980s and early '90s, hint at certain insect shapes, like a praying mantis or spiders, by means of subtle geometric transformations. These compositions were created with the help of an early Amiga computer graphic program, which the artist employed in a typically intuitive way, printing out the eccentric designs and patterns and reconstituting them as three-dimensional maquettes in cardboard and Foamcore.

While attracted to perceptual games, Ginnever is not focused merely on the illusionistic tricks of the composition. His welded parallelograms and triangular elements impart a sense of movement as the angular forms seem to lean against each other at a slant, as if about to collapse to the ground or crawl along in a graceful, slow-motion choreography.

54-57. *Moonwalker I*, 1989 (four views)

29

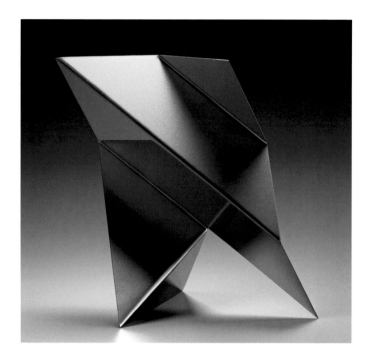

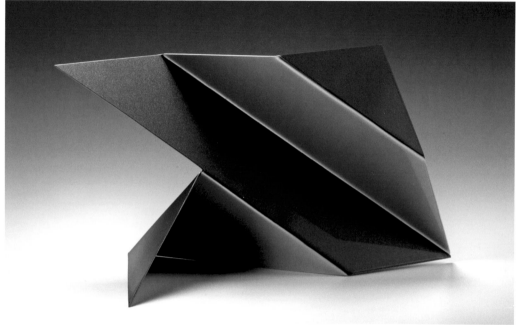

Ginnever continues to make vital work, as evidenced by a recent visit to his home and studio on his sprawling Vermont farm that looks a bit like a sculpture park. Now in his mid-eighties, he is more at ease creating smaller pieces. But in these jewel-like tabletop sculptures in painted aluminum and other sheet metal, he continues to experiment with the hard-edge, folded geometric forms that correspond to the monumental public works for which he is well known. Some of the recent works are part of his ongoing *Origami* series.

The *Origami* pieces first appeared in the 1970s, and the artist continues to create new and ever more vibrant additions to this refined and colorful group, such as *Origami Series I, II,* and *III* (all 2012). Each of these works, rarely more than two or three feet tall, consists of folded aluminum or steel facets painted with highly reflective acrylic lacquer in just two solid colors. Consistent in his approach, Ginnever studied the work of Japanese origami masters, but created his own version of the technique to suit his sculptural vision. He had no wish to follow "the rules" of origami. In Ginnever's *Origami* series, the deceptively simple shapes and brilliant, saturated colors—red/pale green, purple/pink, orange/lavendar—seem playful at first, but the works deliver a surprising and varied emotional charge.

58-59. *Origami Series III* (Unique), 2012 (two views)

OPPOSITE
LEFT, ABOVE/BELOW
60-61. *Origami Series Maquettes,* 2012 (two views)

RIGHT, ABOVE/BELOW
62-63. *Origami Series I* (Unique), 2012 (two views)

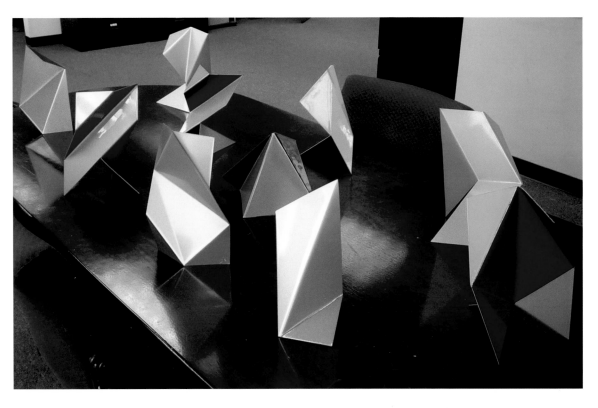
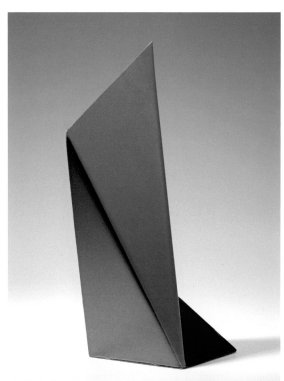

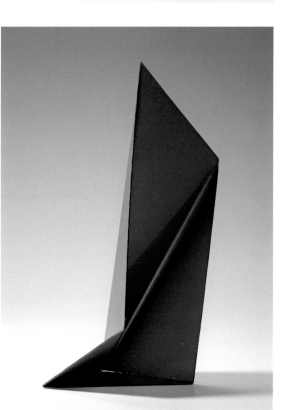

31

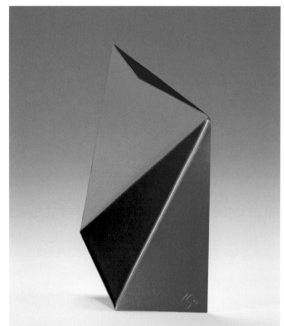

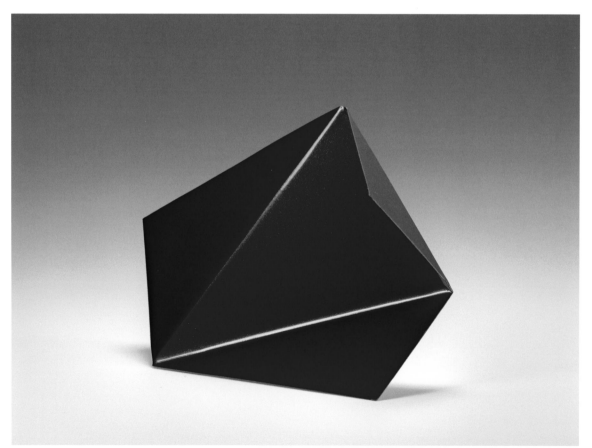

64-67. *Origami Series II* (A/P), 2012 (four views)

The folds in the *Origami* pieces, like those in most of Ginnever's works, seem to be forever unfolding, just as they enfold great expanses of time and space. Ginnever aims to challenge viewers' ideas about visual perception, and to dislodge their long-held assumptions about the nature of space. He has often spoken of his work in relation to the Japanese concept of *ma*: roughly translated as "space" or "pause," *ma* is simultaneous awareness of both form and non-form, with time as a critical element of spatial perception.

The earnest wit and meditative quality in the *Origami* works may be found in nearly everything the artist has produced. In his work, Ginnever offers something seemingly impossible—an awareness of the infinite, or a steadfast feeling of infinity.

DAVID EBONY is a contributing editor of *Art in America*, Artnet news, and Yale University Press online.

Endnotes

1. Gilles Deleuze, *The Fold: Leibniz and the Baroque*, University of Minnesota Press, Minneapolis, 1993, pp. 34–35.

2. This and other Ginnever quotes are taken from the author's conversations with the artist in Vermont, in April, 2014, and in New York City, in December, 2017.

3. See Bruce Nixon's essay in *Charles Ginnever: Rashomon*, Iris & B. Gerald Cantor Center for Visual Arts, Stanford University, Stanford, 2000, p. 13.

4. *Ibid.*, p. 45.

GINNEVER

DAEDALUS

CHARLES GINNEVER'S *Daedalus* is a challenging work. It disturbs comfortable habits of perception and resists our efforts to reconcile what we see with what we know.

We know *Daedalus* to be composed of the simplest of elements: five identical parallelograms of half-inch-thick Cor-Ten steel, each bent on its longer diagonal axis. The five segments differ only in the angles of their respective bends, which range from 90 to 142 degrees.

The arrangement of the five elements within the completed sculpture is equally straightforward. The segment with the right-angle bend lies with two of its four edges resting on the ground. The segment with the next-sharpest bend is adjacent, leaning against the first and supported by it, though in actual contact only at the extreme tip. The remaining segments follow, building one upon the other. They are welded together for added stability, but the entire structure could, in fact, stand by itself, unsupported by welds or braces. The simplicity, clarity and rationality of this arrangement are evident when the scale model of the sculpture is viewed from above.

68. *Daedalus*, 1975
University of Michigan Museum of Art, Ann Arbor

35

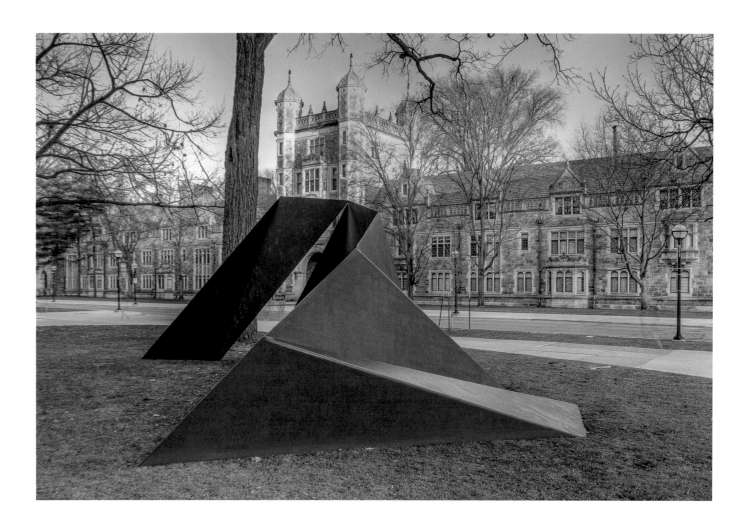

69. *Daedalus*, 1975
University of Michigan Museum of Art, Ann Arbor

Our immediate sensory experience of *Daedalus*, however, is of an entirely different order. Viewed from the ground level, *Daedalus* has a visual complexity that totally confounds our intellectual understanding of its organizational simplicity. The difficulty of reconciling what we see with what we know is compounded by the fact that the way we see the piece is often radically altered by our own movements in relation to it. Shifts of only a few feet transform our impressions. From one vantage point it seems entirely closed, like a steel mountain. From another spot only ten feet away it opens like the spread fingers of a hand.

This changeability, perhaps the sculpture's most striking characteristic, is effectively suggested by Art School student Duane Gall's account of his initial encounter:

…I visited Daedalus Monday night after dinner. I took down a series of impressions of the sculpture as I walked around it, from the first sight on South U. behind the museum, clockwise to the benches and steps in front of the museum's main entrance. The changes I saw took place in time as well as space, since the evening became progressively deeper and the light of the sunset gave way to artificial light. These are the views I had of the sculpture on this particular night …

First glimpse, South University:

I see it emerge slowly and alarmingly (from behind the museum) like the prow of a battleship. It cruises steadily into view, keeping pace with me. Its spiked, armor-plate appearance, from this distance gives the impression that it is part of something very big and forbidding. Soon it stands apart from its surroundings. Now it is self-contained, single, but still forbidding, like a turret.

Closer:

Every panel is a different hue in the twilight—grays (several), black, russet, sky, salmon, ochre, tan. The segments are bunched at one side like parts of a fan half-opened.

From South U. and State:

Ramses, way of the cold, draws his cape around him with a defiant sweep.

From the crosswalk:

A snapshot of breakers. The towering surf slowly spills its bulk forward, crunching onto packed sand.

From State:

A cairn points the way. A door closes.

Walking around:

It pirouettes slowly in a wide stance the way skaters make a turn with toes pointed outward. Car headlights wash up on the panels and run down again as traffic flows around it.

ABOVE/BELOW
70. *Atlantis*, 1976
State University of New York, Buffalo

71. *Olympus*, 1976
The Bradley Foundation, Milwaukee, WI

Cor-Ten steel, the material of which *Daedalus* is made, is itself a variable element. As the steel surface oxidizes, its color changes from a bright, powdery orange to a dark, rich, dense brown. Once the weathering process is completed, the surface seals itself against further corrosion. Should the surface be scratched or scraped, however, the weathering process is repeated and the injury slowly "heals" itself. Three or four years will be required for the sculpture to acquire its ultimate patina.

The name *Daedalus* is rich in literary associations. In Greek mythology, Daedalus was the master craftsman and architect who, according to Ovid, designed the labyrinth in which King Minos of Crete penned up the monstrous Minotaur. Imprisoned himself by the King, Daedalus escaped. Fashioning wings of wax and feathers, he took to the air with his son Icarus and fled the island kingdom. The story of Icarus's foolhardy ascent toward the sun and fatal plunge into the Aegean has been a popular theme with artists for centuries.

Given the clue of the sculpture's title, we find it easy to connect Daedalus with aspects of the ancient myth. To some viewers the monumental structure suggests a skillfully contrived maze; others see a wing-like shape rising and falling, evoking sensations of flight. Since such associations come easily, it seems important to determine the extent to which they may be helpful (or harmful) to a proper understanding of the sculpture itself.

First, it must be understood that the sculpture was in no way intended as an illustration of the Daedalus myth, nor even as a symbolic representation of it. The piece, in fact, was christened only after it and a related, smaller work had been completed. Studying the smaller sculpture, Ginnever never fancied a resemblance to a broken wing. This suggested Icarus's ill-fated flight, and the piece was named accordingly. The larger sculpture—obviously a near relative —thus became *Daedalus*. The Greek names bestowed on these two seminal works set the pattern for a continuing series of related monumental sculptures: *Nautilus*, in the collection of the Walker Art Center in Minneapolis; *Protagoras*, purchased by the General Services Administration for Saint Paul's new Federal Court House; *Atlantis*; *Olympus*; and *Crete*.

In view, then, of the *ex post facto* naming process, is it wrong to associate the museum's sculpture with the story of the father of flight? Not necessarily,

ABOVE
72-73. *Crete*, 1976–78 (two views)
Laumeier Sculpture Park Collection, St. Louis, MO

BELOW
74. *Protagoras*, 1976
Burger Federal Building, St. Paul, MN

39

says Ginnever, provided such literary associations lead us to look more closely and thoughtfully at the work itself. Had he wished, after all, the artist could have chosen a more neutral designation, or assigned his piece a number, or given it no name at all. By naming a work, its maker subtly colors our perception of it. The name *Daedalus* at the very least supports a reading of the sculpture as being in some way possessed of a mythic character, as if it were a kind of iron age Stonehenge marking the sacred site of a vanished people. Such associations are not inimical to a proper understanding of the sculpture if they help us see better what is actually there.

In discussing his work—not just *Daedalus*, but the large and varied body of sculpture he has produced in the course of thirty years—Ginnever frequently describes a form as "breathing." A successful sculpture "breathes." By this he has made reference to the alternate opening and closing, expanding and contracting, that the viewer perceives in moving around the sculpture. It is, perhaps more than anything else, this rhythmic pattern of systole, and diastole that accounts for the extraordinary vitality of *Daedalus*. Ginnever sees this not as something new or unique to his work, but in fact as the traditional central concern of sculpture. The forms may change, but the sculptor's problem remains the same: to make them breathe.

To breathe is to live and to live is to change. Mutability is the one constant feature of Ginnever's work, and *Daedalus* gives striking evidence of the artist's ability to endow a massive, geometric structure with the vitality of a living organism.

The sculpture's chameleon-like transformations, together with its stubbornly egalitarian refusal to acknowledge a single dominant, primary view, make it an extraordinarily difficult piece to hold in mind. When we attempt to visualize a familiar face we nearly always summon up a straight frontal view, a "mug shot," despite the fact that in actuality we see our friends from every possible angle. There is a hierarchy in our impressions, and the full-face view comes first. With *Daedalus*, however, there is no full-face view. The sculpture has no "front" or "back." An adequate mental image would have the character of a film clip—but we habitually visualize in snapshots. Because of the difficulty we experience in forming a clear mental picture of *Daedalus* in the absence of the piece itself

there tends to be a small shock of surprise, a sense of fresh discovery with each encounter.

So thoroughly indoctrinated are we with a conception of three-dimensional space articulated by the conventions of Renaissance perspective that we find it difficult to deal with a form that declines to give us right angles or converging parallels. This is especially true of a piece like *Daedalus*, which at first glance might be taken for a model exercise in Euclidian geometry.

Carter Ratcliff, writing in *Art in America*, has observed:

> *What is striking about Daedalus is its refusal to offer reassurances. Comparisons point up the fact that most geometrical sculpture does reassure us. Specifically, it reassures us about the nature of space of the possibilities for gesture in space. Our space, the space of Western culture, is 'right-angled'—as our architecture, our urban grids, our traditional pictorial systems condition us to assume.*

OPPOSITE
75-77. *Troika II*, 2003 (three views)
JoAnn Sivley Ruppert Collection,
Santa Fe, NM

78. *Daedalus*, 1975
University of Michigan Museum of Art,
Ann Arbor

A comparison of *Daedalus* with Tony Rosenthal's nearby "cube" in Regents' Plaza is instructive. One's first perception of Rosenthal's sculpture even from a considerable distance, is of a giant cube tipped up and resting on one corner. Further exploration only confirms the initial impression. Although each of the six sides is treated differently, the piece does, in fact, essentially conform to our first reading of it as a simple, geometric solid. *Daedalus*, by contrast, offers no easily interpreted profile. One's first impression is a function of the direction from which the piece is approached, and further exploration negates any simple interpretation.

Not only does *Daedalus* present strikingly different aspects from different vantage points, but the piece also is unusually responsive to changes of time and season. In planning the installation, Ginnever took pains to calculate the changing angles of light fall at different times of day and year. *Daedalus* is oriented to take full advantage of these alternations. On sunny days triangular shadows falling on grass or snow, or upon the piece itself, make a subtle, shifting counterpoint to the motionless steel plates.

79. *Daedalus*, 1975
University of Michigan Museum of Art, Ann Arbor

Changes in weather also transform *Daedalus* in ways that seem natural and harmonious. Traditional monuments are at best indifferent to the elements. W. H. Auden's description of a winter's afternoon, when "snow disfigured the public statues," aptly conjures up the slightly ludicrous image of snow-capped and icicle-bedecked bronze effigies of statesmen and soldiers. Even modern, non-representational sculptures often tend to seem at least muffled, if not actually deformed, by accumulations of ice and snow.

Daedalus, by contrast, positively revels in winter's embrace (a fortunate attribute in view of the ample opportunity Michigan's climate affords for such revelry). Thrusting up through a blanket of snow, its blades resemble the jagged ice floes of Caspar David Friedrich's nineteenth-century romantic masterpiece "Artic Shipwreck." Snow powdering the broad backs of the lower segments emphasizes their articulation, accenting contrasts between horizontal and vertical planes. The dark, triangular shapes stand out sharply against the enveloping whiteness.

80. *Daedalus*, 1975
University of Michigan Museum of Art, Ann Arbor

43

44

Our immediate experience of *Daedalus* contradicts our knowledge of it in yet another way: common sense tells us that each of the five steel segments must weigh half-a-ton or more. Each is supported only at its single point of contact with the next lower element. Logically, this should give the whole structure a precarious, house-of-cards quality. The sheer weight of the piece—its obvious potential energy—ought to imbue it with an aura of menace. The actual effect, however, as Carter Ratcliff has observed, "…is of a serenity that is at odds with its size and with the precariousness one might be attempted to associate with its angularity."

The behavior of museum visitors and passers-by provides empirical confirmation of this critical perception. Children clamber up the sloping plates as parents look on approvingly; sunbathers reclining on the lower segments or on the grass nearby; a guitarist performs, sitting cross-legged under the "band shell"; lovers embrace in its shadow. It is evident that no one feels threatened by *Daedalus*. Before the sculpture came no one sat on the museum lawn to study, sunbathe, or picnic. The lawn was *nowhere*; a patch of grass to be traversed on the way to *somewhere*. *Daedalus* has made a place, a site, of what previously was a non-site.

81-82. *Daedalus*, 1975
University of Michigan Museum of Art, Ann Arbor

46

Perhaps this is the ultimate function of public sculpture in our age of increasing environmental homogeneity. As our cities become indistinguishable from one another and each town grows more like every other, we are in danger of losing our sense of identity, our sense of place. *Daedalus*, by powerfully asserting its own individuality, helps secure the uniqueness of one small corner of our urban environment. Though Bernard Berenson doubtless would not have approved of the direction taken by modern sculpture, his insistence that art must be, above all, "life enhancing" is not inappropriate as a requisite for the art of our time. If the ability of a work of art to transform its immediate environment to vitalize a previously inert and characterless space, is an appropriate measure of life enhancement, then *Daedalus* quite clearly meets that requirement.

A. BRET WALLER, Director Emeritus
Indianapolis Museum of Art

Text reprinted from publication, *Daedalus*, celebrating the acquisition of Charles Ginnever's sculpture, *Daedalus* and the University of Michigan Museum of Art's 30th Anniversary Fund. September, 1977. A. Bret Waller served as Director of the University of Michigan Museum of Art, 1973–80.

83-84. *Daedalus*, 1975
University of Michigan Museum of Art, Ann Arbor

GINNEVER

RASHOMON

RASHOMON IS THE COLLECTIVE TITLE Charles [Chuck] Ginnever has given to three related groups of works: an innovative suite of fifteen identical sculptures—open structures of joined and angled steel planes that stand fifteen feet high—each of which can be rotated into a different position; a group of three-foot high maquettes for the identical sculptures, which are individually marked, so that those who exhibit them will know exactly the position each is to be placed in; an artists' book that includes a set of eleven etchings, each depicting a potential position in which the sculpture can be placed.

Ginnever's inspiration for titling these works is the highly acclaimed, award-winning film, *Rashomon* (1950), directed by the great postwar Japanese director, Akira Kurosawa (1910–1998). Based on two short stories by the modernist master, Ryūnosuke Akutagawa (1892–1927), "Rashomon" and "In a Bamboo Grove," the title refers to the immense city gate of Kyoto, where, in the film's opening scene, a woodcutter and a priest are huddled, trying to stay dry during a torrential downpour. The gate is one of the three settings of the film, the other two being a courtyard and a bamboo grove.

85. *Rashomon* (15 units), 1999, Installation, Iowa State University, Ames, 2014

49

Kurosawa decided to work with only three settings due to the small budget he was given by the film company, Daiei, but he also had a formal simplicity in mind, as it might be gleaned from his statement: "I like silent pictures and I always have... I wanted to restore some of this beauty. I thought of it, I remember in this way: one of the techniques of modern art is simplification, and that I must therefore simplify this film."

Accordingly, Kurosawa established three minimalist settings for his collection of untrustworthy characters—a bandit, a woodcutter, a wife and her Samurai husband. Each character gives eyewitness testimony to a magistrate about a rape and a murder in the bamboo grove after the bandit stopped the Samurai and his wife. According to the film critic Stanley Kauffman, Kurosawa often used multiple cameras to film a scene, splicing the various angles together so that the point of view is constantly shifting among the four witnesses. Each narrative is unique while denying the veracity of the others. This multilayered perspective is most likely what inspired Ginnever to give this title to his ambitious project, which was to design a unique sculptural object that can be placed in different and distinct positions, calling to mind Kurosawa's film.

Contradiction and instability lie at the heart of Kurosawa's film—and also of Ginnever's sculptures. Each witness to the crime tells a self-serving story. Is it a coincidence that the unreliable narrators we encounter in *Rashomon* share something with the undependable ones inhabiting Robert Wiene's *The Cabinet of Dr. Caligari* (1920), one of the great German Expressionist films as well as

LEFT/RIGHT

86. Poster for Robert Wiene's 1920 film
The Cabinet of Dr. Caligari
(Das Cabinet des Dr. Caligari)

87. Film still from Robert Wiene's
The Cabinet of Dr. Caligari, 1920

ABOVE, LEFT/RIGHT
88-89. Two scenes from Akira Kurosawa's
1950 film, *Rashomon*

90. Poster for Kurosawa's *Rashomon*

BELOW
91. *Rashomon* (15 units), 1999
Karen and Robert Duncan Collection

one of the most important silent films ever made. Wiene (1873–1938) and Kurosawa were citizens of countries whose deeply rooted nationalist narratives had been destroyed, resulting in catastrophe on every conceivable level. After defeat and humiliation, what narrative could the citizens of these countries believe in?

While it is unlikely that the historical circumstances against which Kurosawa made his film played a role in Ginnever's decision to explore a sculpture's multifarious positional possibilities, I don't think it should be completely ignored either. Instead of a secure and/or repeating form, which is certainly one of the hallmarks of Minimalist sculpture (which can be dated back to Classical and Impressionist sculpture), Ginnever's open, planar abstractions convey a fluid state of instability and change. You begin to feel stuck inside your body, increasingly aware of how little information your eyes are able to perceive

92. *Gyro I*, 1982

52

and process. Rather than verifying what you see and remember, the eyes and mind begin to feel disconnected and unreliable, which is an unsettling state, to say the least.

Through his thorough and thoughtful subversion of long held historical assumptions about sculpture, including the idea that a sculptor should make a significant form, whether organic or industrial, whose placement is fixed, Ginnever comes to occupy a unique position. I am thinking of important, innovative sculptors such as Constantin Brancusi, Isamu Noguchi, Henry Moore, Ruth Asawa, Donald Judd, Mark di Suvero and Richard Serra, all of whom are remembered for making a signature form, something that could be readily grasped. It is this understanding of sculpture that Ginnever successfully challenges, and thus it is in this company that he ultimately belongs.

93-94. *Hangover II*, 1983 (two views)

In his sculptural suite, *Rashomon*, Ginnever defies viewers to visually grasp and remember the sculpture, as we encounter another identical one in a different position in the landscape. What tells us that they are identical? Do we compare the components? Do we rotate them in our minds? In slowing down our experience, and making us question both our eyes and our memory, Ginnever exposes our haste to consume without reflection, to move on to the next thing or experience.

95. *Rashomon* (3 units), 1995
Di Rosa Preserve, Napa, CA

54

96. *Rashomon Sculpture Study V*, 1994

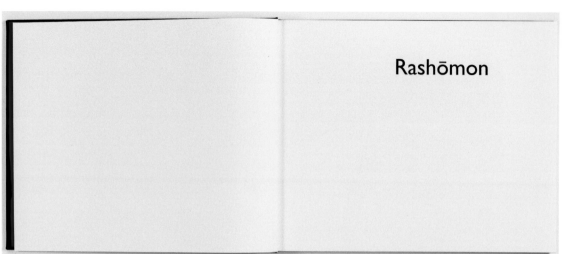

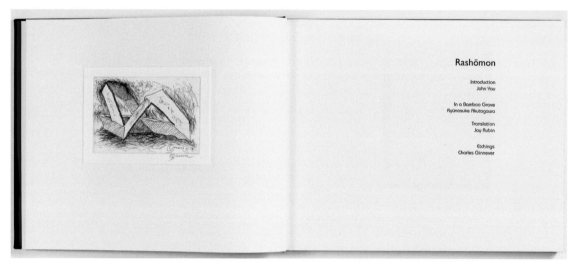

97-102. *Rashomon* (15/40), 2014
Limited-edition artists' book with
etchings and letterpress printing
Karen and Robert Duncan Collection

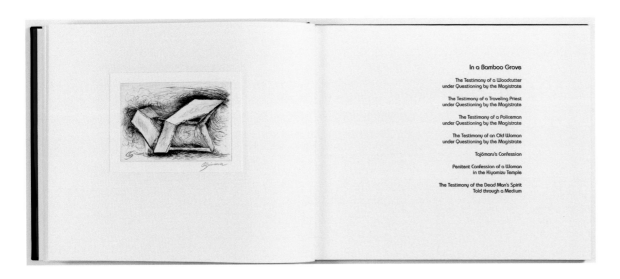

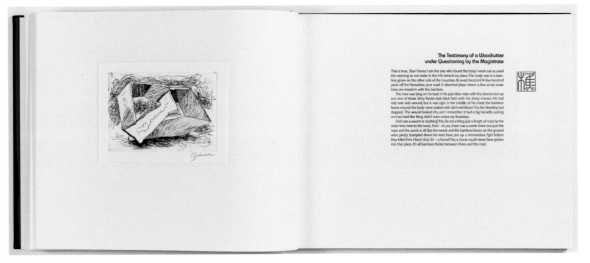

This is where the eleven etchings in the *Rashomon* artists' book come in. Each one registers a different position taken by an object. However, instead of confirming that it is the same object placed differently, the dissimilar views are apt to confound us. Are they really straightforward depictions of the same object? Growing doubtful, we become untrustworthy narrators of our own experience. If each print is of an identical object whose position in space is unique, we become aware of our perceptual and mental limitations, of the challenges presented to the eye and mind. We may even go so far as to feel that our grasp of experience has been eroded.

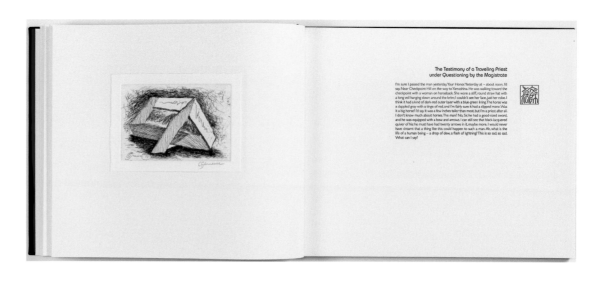

The Testimony of a Traveling Priest
under Questioning by the Magistrate

I'm sure I passed the man yesterday, Your Honor. Yesterday at — about noon, I'd say. Near Checkpoint Hill on the way to Yamashina. He was walking toward the checkpoint with a woman on horseback. She wore a stiff, round straw hat with a long veil hanging down around the brim; I couldn't see her face, just her robe. I think it had a kind of dark-red outer layer with a blue-green lining. The horse was a dappled gray with a tinge of red, and I'm fairly sure it had a clipped mane. Was it a big horse? I'd say it was a few inches taller than most, but I'm a priest after all. I don't know much about horses. The man? No, Sir, he had a good-sized sword, and he was equipped with a bow and arrows. I can still see that black-lacquered quiver of his: he must have had twenty arrows in it, maybe more. I would never have dreamt that a thing like this could happen to such a man. Ah, what is the life of a human being — a drop of dew, a flash of lightning? This is so sad, so sad. What can I say?

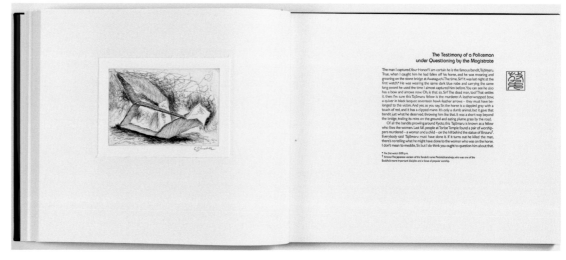

The Testimony of a Policeman
under Questioning by the Magistrate

The man I captured, Your Honor? I am certain he is the famous bandit, Tajōmaru. True, when I caught him he had fallen off his horse, and he was moaning and groaning on the stone bridge at Awataguchi. The time, Sir? It was late night at the first watch.* He was wearing the same dark blue robe and carrying the same long sword he used the time I almost captured him before. You can see he also has a bow and arrows now. Oh, is that so, Sir? The dead man, too? That settles it, then. I'm sure this Tajōmaru fellow is the murderer. A leather-wrapped bow, a quiver in black lacquer, seventeen hawk-feather arrows — they must have belonged to the victim. And yes, as you say, Sir, the horse is a dappled gray with a touch of red, and it has a clipped mane. It's only a dumb animal, but it gave that bandit just what he deserved, throwing him like that. It was a short way beyond the bridge, trailing its reins on the ground and eating plume grass by the road.

Of all the bandits prowling around Kyoto, this Tajōmaru is known as a fellow who likes the women. Last fall, people at Toribe Temple found a pair of worshippers murdered — a woman and a child — on the hill behind the statue of Binzuru.† Everybody said Tajōmaru must have done it. If it turns out he killed the man, there's no telling what he might have done to the woman who was on the horse. I don't mean to meddle, Sir, but I do think you ought to question him about that.

* The first watch: 8:00 p.m.
† Binzuru: The Japanese version of the Sanskrit name Piṇḍolabharadvāja, who was one of the Buddha's more important disciples and a focus of popular worship.

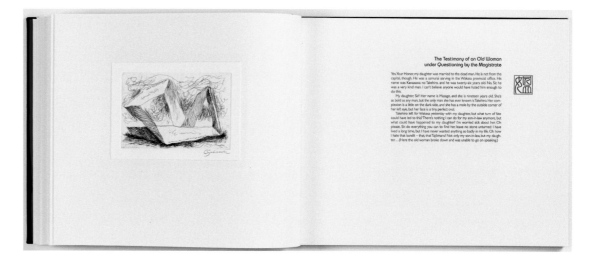

The Testimony of an Old Woman
under Questioning by the Magistrate

Yes, Your Honor, my daughter was married to the dead man. He is not from the capital, though. He was a samurai serving in the Wakasa provincial office. His name was Kanazawa no Takehiro, and he was twenty-six years old. No, Sir, he was a very kind man. I can't believe anyone would have hated him enough to do this.

My daughter? Sir? Her name is Masago, and she is nineteen years old. She's as bold as any man, but the only man she has ever known is Takehiro. Her complexion is a little on the dark side, and she has a mole by the outside corner of her left eye, but her face is a tiny perfect oval.

Takehiro left for Wakasa yesterday with my daughter, but what turn of fate could have led to this? There's nothing I can do for my son-in-law anymore, but what could have happened to my daughter? I'm worried sick about her. Oh please, Sir, do everything you can to find her: leave no stone unturned. I have lived a long time, but I have never wanted anything so badly in my life. Oh how I hate that bandit — that, that Tajōmaru! Not only my son-in-law, but my daughter... (Here the old woman broke down and was unable to go on speaking.)

Tajōmaru's Confession

Sure, I killed the man. But I didn't kill the woman. So, where did she go? I don't know any better than you do. Now, wait just a minute – you can torture me all you want, but I can't tell you what I don't know. And besides, now that you've got me, I'm not going to hide anything. I'm no coward.

I met that couple yesterday a little after noon. The second I saw them, a puff of wind lifted her veil and I caught a peek at her. Just a peek: that's maybe why she looked so perfect to me – an absolute bodhisattva of a woman.[*] I made up my mind right then to take her even if I had to kill the man.

Oh come on, killing a man is not as big a thing as people like you seem to think. If you're going to take somebody's woman, a man has to die. When I kill a man, I do it with my sword, but people like you don't use swords. You gentlemen kill with your power, with your money, and sometimes just with your words: you tell people you're doing them a favor. True, no blood flows, the man is still alive, but you've killed him all the same. I don't know whose sin is greater – yours or mine. (A sarcastic smile.)

Of course, if you can take the woman without killing the man, all the better. Which is exactly what I was hoping to do yesterday. It would have been impossible on the Yamashina post road, of course, so I thought of a way to lure them into the hills.

It was easy. I fell in with them on the road and made up a story. I told them I had found an old burial mound[†] in the hills, and when I opened it, it was full of swords and mirrors and things. I said I had buried the stuff in a bamboo grove on the other side of the mountain to keep anyone from finding out about it, and I'd sell it cheap to the right buyer. He started getting interested soon enough. It's scary what greed can do to people, don't you think? In less than an hour, I was leading that couple and their horse up a mountain trail.

[*] *bodhisattva of a woman: In Mahayana Buddhism an enlightened being who compassionately defers entry into Nirvana in order to help others attain enlightenment. By extension, a perfectly beautiful woman.*

[†] *burial mound: Prehistoric Japanese aristocrats were often buried in mounded graves containing jewels, weapons, and other valuables.*

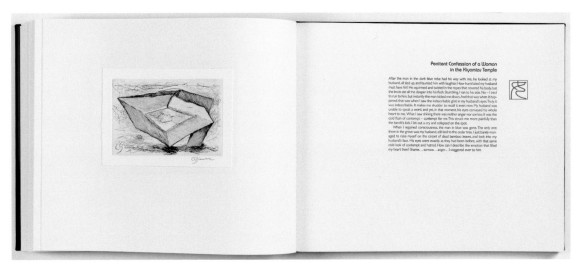

Penitent Confession of a Woman in the Kiyomizu Temple

After the man in the dark blue robe had his way with me, he looked at my husband, all tied up, and taunted him with laughter. How humiliated my husband must have felt! He squirmed and twisted in the ropes that covered his body, but the knots ate all the deeper into his flesh. Stumbling, I ran to his side. No – I tried to run to him, but instantly the man kicked me down. And that was when it happened: that was when I saw the indescribable glint in my husband's eyes. Truly, it was indescribable. It makes me shudder to recall it even now. My husband was unable to speak a word, and yet, in that moment, his eyes conveyed his whole heart to me. What I saw shining there was neither anger nor sorrow. It was the cold flash of contempt – contempt for me. This struck me more painfully than the bandit's kick. I let out a cry and collapsed on the spot.

When I regained consciousness, the man in blue was gone. The only one there in the grove was my husband, still tied to the cedar tree. I just barely managed to raise myself on the carpet of dead bamboo leaves, and look into my husband's face. His eyes were exactly as they had been before, with that same cold look of contempt and hatred. How can I describe the emotion that filled my heart then? Shame... sorrow... anger... I staggered over to him.

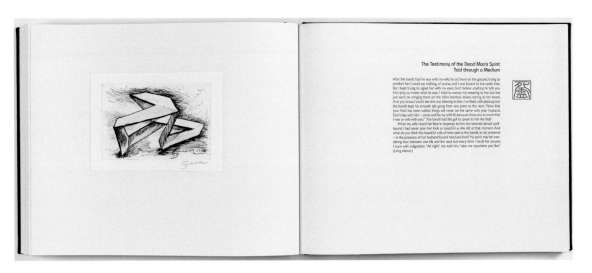

The Testimony of the Dead Man's Spirit Told through a Medium

After the bandit had his way with my wife, he sat there on the ground, trying to comfort her. I could say nothing, of course, and I was bound to the cedar tree. But I kept trying to signal her with my eyes: Don't believe anything he tells you. He's lying, no matter what he says. I tried to convey my meaning to her, but she just went on cringing there on the fallen bamboo leaves, staring at her knees. And, you know, I could see she was listening to him. I writhed with jealousy, but the bandit kept his smooth talk going from one point to the next: "Now that your flesh has been soiled, things will never be the same with your husband. Don't stay with him – come and be my wife! It's because I love you so much that I was so wild with you." The bandit had the gall to speak to her like that!

When my wife raised her face in response to him, she seemed almost spellbound. I had never seen her look so beautiful as she did at that moment. And what do you think this beautiful wife of mine said to the bandit, in my presence – in the presence of her husband bound hand and foot? My spirit may be wandering now between one life and the next, but every time I recall her answer, I burn with indignation. "All right," she told him, "take me anywhere you like." (Long silence.)

103-108. *Rashomon* (15/40), 2014
Limited-edition artists' book with
etchings and letterpress printing
Karen and Robert Duncan Collection

RIGHT
109. *Rashomon Etching – Position 8*, 1994

60

Ginnever has never aspired to an idealized or signature form in his *oeuvre*. Paul Cézanne's belief that the cube, cone, and sphere are irreducible structures underlying all forms holds little meaning for him. Rather, he achieves a condition of music that few of his peers come close to approaching—a sense that change holds sway over everything, including form. And in so doing he makes a significant contribution to sculpture and our understanding of it.

JOHN YAU is an art critic, poet, essayist, and writer based in New York City. He was Arts Editor for *The Brooklyn Rail* (2009–11), and now writes regularly for Hyperallergic.com. He is a Professor of Critical Studies at Mason Gross School of the Arts (Rutgers University).

OPPOSITE
110. *Rashomon Etching – Six Positions*, 1994

111. *Rashomon Sculpture Study VI – Six Positions*, 1995

61

GINNEVER

MULTUS

ON THE TABLE in front of you is a large rectangular sheet of stiff, copper-colored paper—the color recalls the rich patina we find in Charles [Chuck] Ginnever's sculptures. A series of solid and broken lines have been printed on the paper. Together, they form a zigzag going diagonally from one corner to the other. Each series indicates the action that must be undertaken—folding the paper. Nothing gets thrown away.

Together, both sets of lines form a symmetrical shape that lies diagonally within the rectangle, like a giant too big to sleep on the only bed in the house. This is the first clue as to what is going to happen after you follow the simple instructions. A planar object, a lightweight portable sculpture with sharp edges, will emerge from the paper's flat plane.

One of the first things that strikes me about Ginnever's folded and cut print is that it feels both monumental and delicate, a paradox that compels me to look again and again. You might think of origami, the Japanese art of folding paper, but Ginnever has raised that art to new heights. For one thing, *Multus* seems to require so little folding, which is not the case with origami. The other fact is that the object is abstract. Ginnever has fashioned out of a single rectangle

112. *Multus*, 2012

63

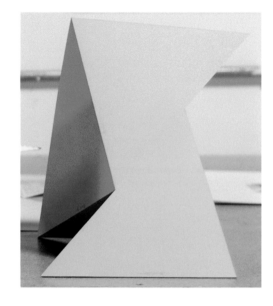

LEFT/RIGHT
113. *Multus* (Maquette), 2012
114. *Multus* (Sheet), 2012

OPPOSITE
115. Instructions for folding *Multus*

64

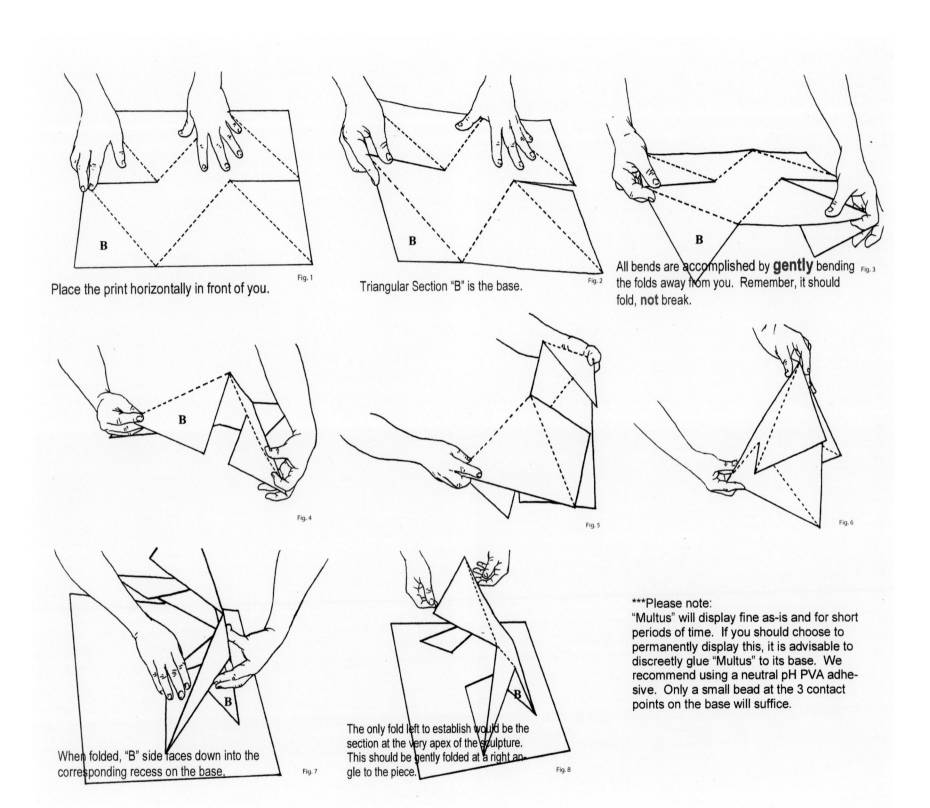

Place the print horizontally in front of you. Fig. 1

Triangular Section "B" is the base. Fig. 2

All bends are accomplished by **gently** bending the folds away from you. Remember, it should fold, **not** break. Fig. 3

Fig. 4

Fig. 5

Fig. 6

When folded, "B" side faces down into the corresponding recess on the base. Fig. 7

The only fold left to establish would be the section at the very apex of the sculpture. This should be gently folded at a right angle to the piece. Fig. 8

***Please note:
"Multus" will display fine as-is and for short periods of time. If you should choose to permanently display this, it is advisable to discreetly glue "Multus" to its base. We recommend using a neutral pH PVA adhesive. Only a small bead at the 3 contact points on the base will suffice.

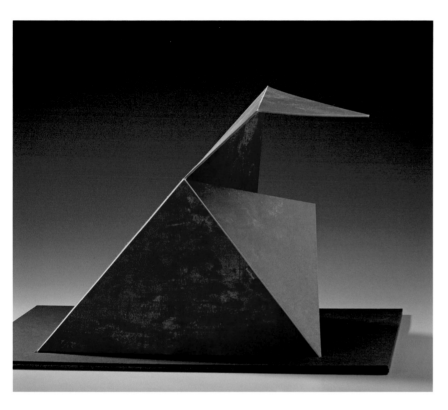
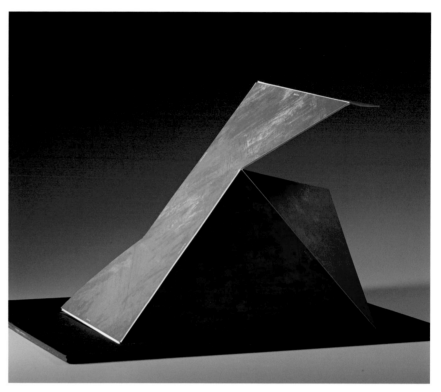
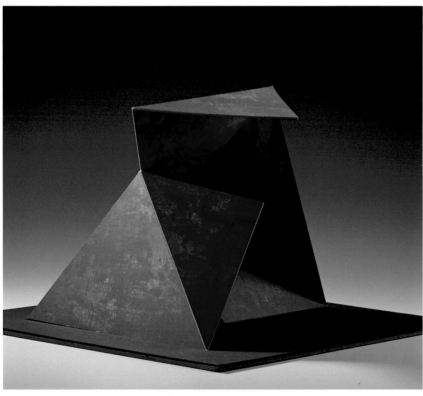
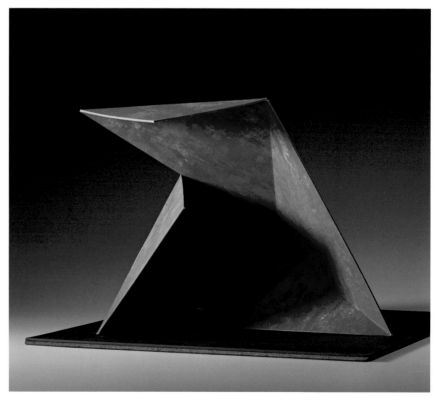

66

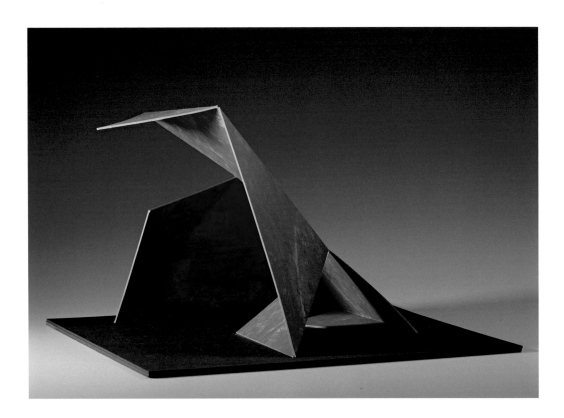

a dance between triangles and pyramids that lifts itself gracefully, like a gymnast, into the air.

The tension between the flat plane and the folded form asks us to pay attention to the everyday world we live in, and to recognize that in the simplest things—a flat sheet of paper—there exists a possibility simultaneously enchanting and revealing. At the core of Ginnever's work exists a state of wonderment.

Ginnever's willingness to be surprised by the simplest things is what makes his work special and exacting. Both literally and metaphorically, there is no other way to make *Multus*. It must be what it is.

JOHN YAU
2012

116-120. *Multus*, 2012 (five views)

GINNEVER

BIOGRAPHY

BIBLIOGRAPHY

SELECTED PUBLIC &
PRIVATE COLLECTIONS

Mirage, 2005

BIOGRAPHY

BORN

1931   San Mateo, California

EDUCATION

1949–51   San Mateo Junior College, San Mateo, CA, A.A.

1953   Alliance Francaise, Paris, France

1954   Universitá per Stranieri, Perugia, Italy

1953–55   Académie de la Grande Chaumière, Paris, France, under Ossip Zadkine

1955   Atelier 17, Paris, France, under Stanley W. Hayter

1955–57   California School of Fine Arts (San Francisco Art Institute), San Francisco, CA, B.A. 1957

1957–59   Cornell University, Ithaca, NY, M.F.A. 1959

Chuck Ginnever working at Landfall Press,
Santa Fe, NM, 2012

TEACHING

1957–59	Cornell University, Ithaca, NY
1963	Pratt Institute, Brooklyn, NY
1964	The New School for Social Research, New York, NY
1964–65	Brooklyn Museum School, Brooklyn, NY
1965	Newark School of Fine and Industrial Art, Newark, NJ
1966	Dayton Art Institute, Dayton, OH, Artist-in-Residence
	Aspen School of Contemporary Art, Aspen, CO, Head of Sculpture Department, Summer Session
	Orange County Community College, Middletown, NY, Fall
1967–75	Windham College, Putney, VT, Head of Art Department, 1970–71
1974	Hobart School of Welding Technology Summer Sculpture Program, Troy, OH
1987	Vermont Studio School, Johnson, VT, Summer
1989	University of California, Berkeley, CA, Visiting Artist, Winter
1996	Vermont Studio Center, Johnson, VT, Visiting Professor, Summer

AWARDS

1957	California School of Fine Arts, San Francisco, CA, Sculpture Award
1974	John Simon Guggenheim Fellowship
1975	National Endowment for the Arts, Individual Artist Grant
1998	Pollock-Krasner Foundation Grant
1999–2001	Lee Krasner Foundation, Lifetime Achievement Award
2004	Pollock/Krasner Foundation Emergency Grant
	Gottlieb Foundation Emergency Grant
2007	Vermont Art Council, Walter Cerf Award for Lifetime Achievement

COMMISSIONS

1972	Vermont State Council on the Arts, *4 the 5th (of Beethoven)*, on exhibit at Southern Vermont Art Center
1976	General Services Administration, Commission for St. Paul Courthouse, St. Paul, MN, *Protagoras*
	National Endowment for the Arts, Commission for Walker Art Center, Minneapolis, MN, *Nautilus*
1977	Knox Foundation Sculpture Competition for the City of Houston, TX, *Pueblo Bonito*
	National Endowment for the Arts Commission for the University of Michigan, Ann Arbor, MI, *Daedalus*
1978	State University of New York, Albany, NY, *Koronos*
	University of Houston, Houston, TX, *Troika*
1979	Virlane Foundation, K & B Plaza, New Orleans, LA, *The Bird (for Charlie Parker)*
1980	Dayton Art Institute and the City Beautiful Council, Dayton, OH, *Movin' Out (for Jesse Owens)*
	Kanawa Arts Alliance and the National Endowment for the Arts, Charleston, WV, *Charleston Arch*
1981	State University of New York, Buffalo, NY, *Atlantis*
1983	Hurd Development Corporation, Dallas, TX, *Pisa*
1985	Hewlett-Packard Corporation, Palo Alto, CA, *Untitled (In Homage to My Father)*
1987	Koll-Bernal Associates, Pleasanton, CA, *Squared II*
1996	APEC Sculpture Garden, Manila, Philippines, President's Choice, U.S. gift, *Nike*
2005	Voigt Family Foundation, Geyserville, CA, *Zip*
2015	City of San Mateo, CA, *San Mateo Bridge*

72

SCULPTURE DANCES/PERFORMANCES

1961 Graffiti & Animation, 16mm film/video, *Peter Forakis/
Charles Ginnever*

1962 *Ergo Suits Carnival*, Woodstock and Bridgehampton, NY

1963 *Fluxus Festival*, George Segal Farm, New Brunswick, NJ

1966 The Dayton Art Institute, Dayton, OH

1969 *Windham Carnival*, Windham College, Putney, VT

SOLO EXHIBITIONS

1961 Allan Stone Gallery, New York, NY

1965 Bennington College, Bennington, VT

1968 New York Loft, New York, NY, *10 Downtown*

Washington Square Park, New York, NY

1970 Battery Park, New York, NY (on extended exhibit)

Paula Cooper Gallery, New York, NY

1971 Paula Cooper Gallery, New York, NY

1972 Dag Hammarskjold Plaza Sculpture Garden, New York, NY

Paula Cooper Gallery, New York, NY

1975 Sculpture Now, Inc., New York, NY, *Charles Ginnever,
20 Years–20 Works.* Catalogue

1978 Max Hutchinson Gallery, Houston, TX

Max Hutchinson Gallery, New York, NY

Smith Andersen Gallery, Palo Alto, CA

Long Beach Museum of Art, Long Beach, CA

Galerie Simonne Stern, New Orleans, LA,
Charles Ginnever—Metal Sculpture

1979 ConStruct, Chicago, IL

1980 Storm King Art Center, Mountainville, NY. Catalogue

Max Hutchinson Gallery, New York, NY

1981 ConStruct, Chicago, IL, *Charles Ginnever: New Sculpture*,
April 3–May 23

1983 Marlborough Gallery, New York, NY, *Charles Ginnever: Large
Scale Sculpture*, May 7–July 2. Catalogue

1984 Fuller Goldeen Gallery, San Francisco, CA, February 15–
March 10

Lee Park, Dallas, TX, *Charles Ginnever: Large Scale Sculpture*,
March–September

Hurd Development, Dallas, TX, May–August

1986 Fuller Goldeen Gallery, San Francisco, CA, *Charles Ginnever:
New Bronze Sculpture*, June 11–July 3

Sculpture Fields, Kenoza Lake, NY, *Charles Ginnever: Large
Scale Sculpture.* Catalogue

1987 Esprit Sculpture Garden, San Francisco, CA, *Charles Ginnever:
Large Scale Sculpture*, May 4–October

Dorothy Goldeen Gallery, Santa Monica, CA, *Charles Ginnever:
Bronze and Steel Sculpture*, October 14–November 7

1989 Gerald Peters Gallery, Santa Fe, NM, *Charles Ginnever:
Bronze and Steel*, October 13–November 3

1990 Dorothy Goldeen Gallery, Santa Monica, CA, *Charles
Ginnever: Bronze Sculpture*, August 4–September 1

1991 Gerald Peters Gallery, Santa Fe, NM, *Charles Ginnever*,
October 10–November 3

1995 Smith-Andersen Gallery, Palo Alto, CA, *Charles Ginnever:
Sculptures & Etchings*, January 12–February 15

1997 Academy of Art College, San Francisco, CA, *Charles Ginnever:
Sculpture*, February 16–March 22

1999 Iris and B. Gerald Cantor Center for Visual Arts, Stanford
University, Stanford, CA, *Rashomon*

2001 Brian Gross Fine Art, San Francisco, CA, *Charles Ginnever:
Recent Sculpture*, May 3–June 2

2002 Brattleboro Museum, Brattleboro VT, *Charles Ginnever Sculpture*

2003 MOVA (Museum of Visual Art), Luther Burbank Center, Santa
Rosa, CA, *Charles Ginnever Sculpture*, May 2003–May 2005

Fields Sculpture Park, ART OMI, Ghent, NY, *Charles Ginnever
Sculpture*, July 2003–Spring 2005

2004 Wooster Art Space, New York, NY, *Charles Ginnever*

2012 San Jose Institute of Contemporary Art, San Jose, CA, *Charles
Ginnever: Rashomon*, November 17, 2012–February 16, 2013

2013   Montalvo Arts Center, Saratoga, CA, *Charles Ginnever: Rashomon*,
        March 13–September 15

        Riverside Park, New York, NY, *Charles Ginnever: High Rise and
        Medusa*, 2013–14

2014   Center for Contemporary Arts, Santa Fe, NM, *New Perspectives:
        Chuck Ginnever*, August 22–November 2

2018   Clarinda Carnegie Art Museum, Clarinda, IA, *Charles [Chuck]
        Ginnever: Folded Forms*, June 24–December 4. Catalogue

SELECTED GROUP EXHIBITIONS

1955   The Six Gallery, San Francisco, CA

        San Francisco Museum of Art, San Francisco, CA, *Sculpture and
        Drawing Annual*

1956   San Francisco Museum of Art, San Francisco, CA, *Bay Area
        Sculpture*

        The Six Gallery, San Francisco, CA

        San Francisco Museum of Art, San Francisco, CA, *Sculpture
        and Drawing Annual*

1957   Richmond Art Center, Richmond, CA, *Sculpture Annual*

        The Six Gallery, San Francisco, CA

1958   Spatsa Gallery, San Francisco, CA

1960   Martha Jackson Gallery, New York, NY, *New Forms, New Media,
        Parts I & II*. Catalogue

1961   Andrew Dickson White Museum, Cornell University, Ithaca, NY,
        Young New York Artists

1963   Riverside Museum, New York, NY, *10 New York Artists*

        Provincetown, MA, two-man show

1964   Park Place Gallery, New York, NY

1965   Los Angeles County Museum of Art, Los Angeles, CA

        American Federation of the Arts, *Color Sculpture*. Travel through
        1966

        American Express Pavilion, New York World's Fair, Flushing, NY,
        *ART '65—Lesser Known and Unknown Painters, Young American
        Sculpture*. Catalogue

1966   Park Place Gallery, New York, NY, Two-artist exhibition

        Park Place Gallery, New York, NY

1967   Gracie Mansion, New York, NY, *Sculpture in Environment.*

1968   Pucker Gallery, Charles A. Dana Creative Art Center, Colgate
        University, Hamilton, NY, *10 Downtown*. Catalogue

        Paula Cooper Gallery, New York, NY, *Group Show*

1969   Paula Cooper Gallery, New York, NY, *Group Show*

1970   Indianapolis Museum of Art, Indianapolis, IN

        New Gallery, Cleveland, OH

        Paula Cooper Gallery, New York, NY, *Group Show*

1971   Paramus, NJ, *Sculpture in the Park*

1972   Greenwich Library, Greenwich, CT, *New York Artists from the Paula
        Cooper Gallery*

1974   Sculpture Now, Inc., New York, NY, through January 1975

1976   New Orleans Museum of Art, New Orleans, LA, *Fine Arts in
        Federal Buildings*, organized by the General Services
        Administration. Catalogue

        Walker Art Center, Minneapolis, MN, *Sculpture Made in Place—Dill,
        Ginnever, Madsen*. Catalogue

        Central City Park, Atlanta, GA

        Greenwich Arts Council, Greenwich, CT, *Sculpture '76*. Catalogue

        Nassau County Museum of Fine Arts, Roslyn, NY, *Nine Sculptors—
        On the Ground, In the Water, Off the Wall*

1977   John Weber Gallery, New York, NY, *Drawings for Outdoor Sculpture
        1946–1977*. Travel: Mead Art Gallery, Amherst, MA; University of
        California Art Galleries, Santa Barbara, CA; La Jolla Museum of
        Contemporary Art, La Jolla, CA; Hayden Gallery, Massachusetts
        Institute of Technology, Cambridge, MA. Catalogue

        Wave Hill Sculpture Garden, Bronx, NY, *Inaugural Exhibition*

        Sculpture Now, Inc., New York, NY, *Sculpture Yesterday/Today: Mark
        di Suvero, Tom Doyle, Peter Forakis, Charles Ginnever*. Catalogue.

        Washington State University, Pullman, WA, *Two Decades 1957–
        1977, American Sculpture from Northwest Collections*

1978   Max Hutchinson Gallery, Houston, TX

Sculpture Now, Inc., New York, NY, and Herbert F. Johnson Museum of Art, Cornell University, Ithaca, NY, *Cornell Then, Sculpture Now*. Catalogue

1979   Lake George Arts Project, Lake George, NY, *Prospect Mountain Sculpture Show, An Homage to David Smith*. Catalogue

Laumeier Sculpture Park, St. Louis, MO, *Beginnings*

University of Wisconsin, Oshkosh, WI

ConStruct, Chicago, IL, *Group Show*

ConStruct traveling exhibition, *Mark di Suvero, Charles Ginnever, John Henry, Linda Howard, Lyman Kipp, Frank McGuire, Jerry Peart*. Travel through 1981: The Fine Arts Museum of Long Island, Hempstead, NY; Grant Park, Chicago, IL; The Arts Festival of Atlanta, Atlanta, GA; Shidoni Gallery, Tesuque, NM. Catalogue

1980   Traveling exhibition to museums throughout 1981, *Reality of Illusion*

ConStruct, Chicago, IL, *Group Show*

New Orleans, LA, *Contemporary American Sculpture,* through 1981

The Hyde Collection, Glen Falls, NY, *Sculptors' Studies: The Prospect Mountain Sculpture Show*

Sun Gallery, Hayward, CA, *Sculpture*

ConStruct, Chicago, IL, *Group Drawing Show*

Max Hutchinson Gallery, New York, NY, *10 Abstract Sculptures, 1940–1980*

ConStruct Outdoor Travelling Exhibition sponsored by Interpace Corporation, *American Eight*. Travel through 1981: Museum of American Art, New Britain, CT; Memorial Art Gallery, Rochester, NY; Interpace Corporation Headquarters, Parsippany, NJ; Ashland College, Ashland, OH. Catalogue

National Collection of Fine Arts, Smithsonian Institution, Washington, DC, *Across the Nation, Fine Art for Federal Buildings, 1972–1979*. Travel. Catalogue

Middendorf/Lane Gallery, Washington, DC, *The Sculptors of ConStruct: ConStruct Small Scale Travelling Exhibition.* Travel: University of North Dakota, Grand Forks, ND; Columbus, IN

Philbrook Art Center, Tulsa, OK

1981   Max Hutchinson Gallery, New York, NY, *Sculptors' Drawings, Maquettes, and Proposals*

Tallgrass/Crown Center, Kansas City, MO, *10: A Spectrum*

Quay Gallery, San Francisco, CA, *Sculptors' Work on Paper,* November 3–28

City of Cleveland, OH, *Sculpture Outside in Cleveland*. Catalogue

Grand Palais, Paris, France, *FIAC Art Fair*

Park West Galleries, Southfield, MI, from Max Hutchinson Gallery, New York, NY, *Sculpture Now: Contemporary American Sculpture*, November 19, 1981–January 15, 1982

1982   Chicago Art Fair, Chicago, IL, *Mile of Sculpture*, May

Palo Alto Cultural Center, Mitchell Park, Palo Alto, CA, *Palo Alto Outdoor Sculpture Invitational*, June 15, 1982–June 30, 1983

Laumeier Sculpture Park, St. Louis, MO

Fort Mason, San Francisco, CA, *Public Sculpture/Public Sites*

John Berggruen Gallery, San Francisco, CA, *Aspects of Sculpture*

ConStruct Sculpture Park, North Miami, FL, November 21, 1982–Spring 1983

1983   Metropolitan Museum and Art Center, Coral Gables, FL, *ConStruct South*, January 16–March 15

Chicago, IL, *Chicago Sculpture International: Mile 2*, May. Catalogue

Virginia Museum of Fine Arts, Richmond, VA, *Sculpture in the Garden*, August 10, 1983–August 10, 1984

Nassau County Museum of Fine Art, Roslyn, NY, *Sculpture: The Tradition in Steel*, October 9, 1983–January 22, 1984. Catalogue

Max Hutchinson Gallery, New York, NY, *Varieties of Sculptural Ideas: Drawings and Maquettes*, December 22, 1983–January 28, 1984

ConStruct Sculpture Park, North Miami, FL, *ConStruct Group Show*

1984   Miami-Dade Community College Gallery, Miami, FL, *ConStruct*, March 8–29

Robert Hull Fleming Museum, University of Vermont, Burlington, VT, *Contemporary Artists in Vermont*, September 25–December 30

Marlborough Gallery, New York, NY, *Masters of Modern and Contemporary Sculpture*, November 8–December 4

Diane Brown Gallery, New York, NY, *The Success of Failure*, December 12, 1984–January 12, 1985

1985 American Academy and Institute of Arts and Letters, New York, NY, *Paintings and Sculpture by Candidates for Art Awards*, March 4–31

1986 Fuller Goldeen Gallery, San Francisco, CA, *Los Angeles Contemporary Art Fair*, Los Angeles, CA, December 3–5

The Art Store Gallery, Oakland, CA, *Shoebox Show*, December 11, 1986– January 15, 1987

1987 Laumeier Sculpture Park, St. Louis, MO, *The Success of Failure*, February 15–March 29. Travel by Independent Curators, Inc.: University Art Gallery, North Texas State University, Denton, TX, August 31–September 25; Johnson Gallery, Middlebury College, Middlebury, VT, October 25–December 13; University of Arizona Museum of Art, Tucson, AZ, January 31–March 12, 1988. Catalogue

Cold Spring Laboratory, Cold Spring Harbor, NY, *Nothing But Steel*, June 1, 1987–March 31, 1988

Anchorage Museum of History and Art, Anchorage, AK, *Sculpture: Looking Into Three Dimensions*, June 28, 1987–May 29, 1988. Travel: Alaska State Museum, Juneau, AK, July 1–August 7, 1988; University of Alaska Museum, Fairbanks, AK, August 19–October 16, 1988. Catalogue

Anne Reed Gallery, Ketchum, ID, June 29–October 1

Seattle Art Museum, Seattle, WA, *Recent Modern Acquisitions*, August 27–October 18

Dorothy Goldeen Gallery, Santa Monica, CA, *Gallery Artists*, September 10–October 10

1988 Walnut Creek Civic Arts Gallery, Walnut Creek, CA, *Bay Area Bronze*, January 13–March 12

Palo Alto Cultural Center, Palo Alto, CA, *Bay Area Sculpture: Metal, Stone and Wood*, February 21–April 24

Sheehan Gallery, Whitman College, Walla Walla, WA, *Cast in Walla Walla*, November 14–December 16

Dorothy Goldeen Gallery, Santa Monica, CA, *Private Reserve*, December 1–31

1989 Sabbeth Art Gallery, Wunsch Arts Center, Glen Cove, NY, *A Salute to the Gateway Public Sculpture*, August 4–13

Anne Reed Gallery, Ketchum, ID, *Sculpture: Visions Transformed*, July 1–August 1

1990 Socrates Sculpture Park, Long Island City, NY, *Opening Celebration*, April 8–October 15

Marvin Seline Gallery, Houston, TX, *From California*, April 21–May 19

Anne Reed Gallery, Ketchum, ID, *Sculpture: Visions Transformed II*, July 6–August 4

1991 Natsoulas/Novelozo Gallery, Davis, CA, *The Spatsa Gallery: 1958–1961*, January 11–February 3. Catalogue

Dorothy Goldeen Gallery, Santa Monica, CA, *Monochrome*, March 31–May 11

Anne Reed Gallery, Ketchum, ID, *Sculpture: Visions Transformed III*, July 5–August 9

Andre Emmerich Gallery, New York, NY, *Table Sculpture*, July 8–August 16

1992 Ann Jaffe Gallery, Bay Harbor, FL, *27 Anniversary Show*, January 7–31

Gallery Camino Real, Boca Raton, FL, *Bronze*, January 16–February 8

Andre Emmerich Gallery, New York, NY, *Table Sculpture*, May 2–June 26

Anne Reed Gallery, Ketchum, ID, *Visions Transformed IV*, July 8–August 5

1993 Anne Reed Gallery, Ketchum, ID, March 5–April 15

Contract Design Center, San Francisco, CA, *Line, Mass, Process*, March 4–May 31

1995 The Sculpture Gallery, San Francisco, CA, *Selected Artists/Selected Works*, January 19–March 7

Anne Reed Gallery, Ketchum, ID, August 1–31

Palo Alto Cultural Center, Palo Alto, CA, *Concept in Form: Artists' Sketchbooks & Maquettes*, October 5, 1995–January 7, 1996

1998 Gerald Peters Gallery, Santa Fe, NM, *Rashomon*

2001   Chicago Pier, Chicago, IL, *Pier Walk 2001*

2002   Chelsea Studio Gallery, New York, NY, *Unforgettable* (Ground Zero
        Proposals)

        Wright State University Art Galleries, Dayton, OH, *With a View
        Toward the Public*, April 7–May 5. Catalogue

2004   Gerald Peters Gallery, Santa Fe, NM, *Sculpture and Prints*,
        December 10, 2004–January 29, 2005

        National Academy, New York, NY, *179th Annual Exhibition*

2006   Wooster Art Space, New York, NY

2007   Broadbent Gallery, London, England, *Sculpture/Drawing Show—
        Willard Boepple, Charles Ginnever and John Henry*, February
        2–March 3

2009   Allan Stone Gallery, New York, NY, *Bay Area to New York*, October
        28–December 22

2016   Paradise Ridge Ranch, Santa Rosa, CA, *Geometric Reflections*,
        through April 2017

Charles Ginnever: Rashomon, San Jose Institute of Contemporary Art, 2012

BIBLIOGRAPHY

ARTISTS' BOOKS

Akutagawa, Ryūnosuke. Introduction by John Yau. *Rashomon.* Limited-edition artists' book
that includes the story "In a Bamboo Grove" by Ryūnosuke Akutagawa, based on a
twelfth-century Japanese tale, translated by Jay Ruben; eleven etchings by Charles
Ginnever printed by the fellows of the Landfall Institute of the Graphic Arts, Landfall
Press, Santa Fe, NM; letterpress printing and binding designed and executed by Lawrence
G. Van Velzer and Peggy Gotthold at Foolscap Press, Santa Cruz, CA, 2014.

BOOKS

Albright, Thomas. *Art in the San Francisco Bay Area, 1945–1980.* Berkeley, CA: University
of California Press, 1985.

Andersen, Wayne. *American Sculpture in Process, 1930–1970.* Boston, MA: New York
Graphic Society, 1975.

Barros, Ricardo. *Facing Sculpture.* Morrisville, PA: Image Spring Press, 2004.

Boettger, Suzaan. *Earthworks: Art and the Landscape of the Sixties.* Berkeley and Los Angeles,
CA: University of California Press, 2003.

Collischan, Judy. *Welded Sculpture of the Twentieth Century.* New York, NY: Hudson Hills
Press; and Purchase, NY: Neuberger Museum of Art, 2000.

Chuck Ginnever at Landfall Press with Jack Lemon
and Steve Campbell, 2012

Fisher, Doris, and Fisher, Donald. *The Fisher Collection*. San Francisco, CA: Doris and Donald Fisher, 2007.

Harper, Glen, and Moyer, Twylene (eds). *A Sculpture Reader: Contemporary Sculpture Since 1980*. Washington DC. ISC Press, 2006.

_____. *Conversations on Sculpture*. Washington, DC: ISC Press; and Seattle, WA: University of Washington Press, 2007.

Judd, Donald. *The Complete Writings of Donald Judd*. Halifax, Nova Scotia: Press of the Nova Scotia College of Art and Design; New York, NY: New York University Press, 1975.

Krantz, Les. *The New York Art Review*. Chicago, IL: American References Publishing, 1988.

Kuspit, Donald. *Redeeming Art: Critical Reveries*. New York, NY: Allworth Press, 2000.

Leibowitz, J. R. *Hidden Harmony, The Connected Worlds of Physics and Art*. Baltimore, MD: The Johns Hopkins University Press, 2008.

Morris Little, Carol. *A Comprehensive Guide to Outdoor Sculpture in Texas*. Austin, TX: University of Texas Press, 1996.

Stern, H. Peter, and Collen, David. *Sculpture at Storm King*. New York, NY: Abbeville Press Inc., 1980.

Yale University Press. *Socrates Sculpture Park*. Princeton, NJ: Yale University Press, 2006.

CATALOGUES

Alloway, Lawrence, and Kaprow, Allan. Foreword by Martha Jackson. *New Forms—New Media I*. New York, NY: Martha Jackson Gallery, 1960. Photographs by Rudolph Burchkardt.

Andersen, Wayne, and O'Doherty, Brian. *Art '65*. Flushing, NY: American Express Pavilion, New York World's Fair, 1965.

Anderson, Lydia; Moss, Jacqueline; and Rubin, Ida E. (Eds.). *Sculpture 76*. Greenwich, CT: Greenwich Arts Council, 1976.

Angel, Brian. Foreword to *ICAF/LA86: The International Contemporary Art Fair, Los Angeles*. Los Angeles, CA: ICAF/LA86 and Andry Montgomery California, Inc., 1986.

Brown, J. Carter. Preface to *Sculpture at Storm King*. Mountainville, NY: Storm King Art Center, 1980. Photography by David Finn.

Bryant, Edward. *10 Downtown*. Hamilton, NY: Pucker Gallery, Charles A. Dana Creative Arts Center, Colgate University, 1968.

Chicago International Art Exposition. *Chicago International Art Exposition, 1990*. Chicago, IL: Chicago International Art Exposition, 1990.

Cohen, Ronny H. Introduction by Pierre Restany. *Charles Ginnever*. San Francisco, CA: Anne Kohs & Associates, Inc., 1987. Photography by M. Lee Fatherree.

Collischan, Judy. *Neuberger Museum of Art 1997 Biennial Exhibition of Public Art*. Purchase, NY: Neuberger Museum of Art, Purchase, 1997.

Denton, Monroe. *No Man's Land*. New York, NY: Socrates Sculpture Park, 1991.

Emmerich, Andre. *Sculpture Out of Doors*. New York, NY: Andre Emmerich Gallery, 1989.

Fisher, Joel. *The Success of Failure*. New York, NY: Independent Curators, 1987.

FitzGibbons, Ann. *Sculpture: Looking into Three Dimensions*. Anchorage, AK: Anchorage Museum of History and Art, 1987.

Friedman, Nathaniel, and Singer, Clifford. *Art & Mathematics 2000*. New York, NY: The Cooper Union for the Advancement of Science & Art, 2000.

Goldeen, Dorothy. *American Eight*. Parsippany, NJ: Corporate Headquarters, Interpace Corporation; Ashland, OH: Ashland College, 1980.

Hinson, Tom E., and Lockhart, Anne I. *Sculpture Outside in Cleveland*. Cleveland, OH: New Organization for the Visual Arts (NOVA), 1981.

Hobbs, Robert. *Cornell Then, Sculpture Now*. Ithaca, NY: Herbert F. Johnson Museum of Art, Cornell University; New York, NY: Sculpture Now, Inc., 1977.

Katsive, David H. *Mark di Suvero, Charles Ginnever, John Henry, Linda Howard, Lyman Kipp, Frank McGuire, Jerry Peart*. Hempstead, NY: Fine Arts Museum of Long Island, 1979.

Maggini, Mary. *Ginnever*. Woodside, CA: Runnymede Sculpture Farm, 1993.

McCormick, Thomas. *Chicago Sculpture International: Mile 2*. Chicago, IL: Chicago International Sculpture Exhibition, 1983.

Meyer, Ruth K. *Quintessence*. Dayton, OH: City Beautiful Council, 1980.

Nathanson, Carol A. *With a View Toward the Public: Dayton's Alternative Spaces Residence Program, 1977–1983*. Dayton, OH: Wright State University Art Galleries, 2002.

New Orleans Museum of Art. *Fine Arts in the Federal Buildings*. New Orleans, LA: New Orleans Museum of Art, 1976.

Nierengarten-Smith, Beej. Introduction to *Laumeier Sculpture Park: First Decade, 1976–1986*. St. Louis, MO: Laumeier Sculpture Park, 1986.

Nixon, Bruce. *Charles Ginnever: Rashomon*. Stanford, CA: The Iris & B. Gerald Cantor Center for Visual Arts, Stanford University, 2000.

Parente, Janice, and Stigliano, Phyliss. *Sculpture: The Tradition in Steel*. Roslyn, NY: Nassau County Museum of Fine Art, 1983.

Ratcliff, Carter. *Charles Ginnever: Larger-Scale Sculpture*. New York, NY: Marlborough Gallery, 1983.

Sandler, Irving. *The Prospect Mountain Sculpture Show, An Homage to David Smith*. Lake George, NY: Lake George Arts Project, Inc., 1979.

Sculpture Now. *Charles Ginnever: 20 Years—20 Works*. New York, NY: Sculpture Now, Inc., 1975.

Shapiro, David. *Drawings for Outdoor Sculpture 1946–1977*. New York, NY: John Weber Gallery, 1977.

_____. *The Success of Failure*. New York, NY: Diane Brown Gallery, 1984.

Socrates Sculpture Park. *No Man's Land*. New York, NY: Socrates Sculpture Park, 1990.

Squiers, Carol. *Sculpture Yesterday/Today*. New York, NY: Sculpture Now, Inc., 1977.

Storm King Art Center. *Charles Ginnever*. Mountainville, NY: Storm King Art Center, 1980. Photography by Harold Feinstein.

Taylor, Joshua C. *Across the Nation, Fine Art for Federal Buildings, 1972–1979*. Washington, DC: Smithsonian Institution Press, 1980.

Waller, A. Bret. *Daedalus*. Ann Arbor, MI: The University of Michigan Museum of Art, 1977–78.

Selected catalogues of
Chuck Ginnever's work

BROCHURES

Donadio, Emmie. *Contemporary Artists in Vermont*. Burlington, VT: Robert Hull Fleming Museum, University of Vermont, 1984.

Freedman, Doris C. *Walking Tour of Public Art in Lower Manhattan*. New York, NY: The Public Arts Council/Municipal Art Society and Lower Manhattan Cultural Council, 1977.

Hixon, Nancy, and Shaw, Kim. *Art on Campus*. Houston, TX: University of Houston, University Park, 1986.

U.S. General Services Administration. *Art-in-Architecture Program*. Washington, DC: U.S. General Services Administration, 1978.

ARTICLES

Abbe, Mary. "Reinstallation of a St. Paul sculpture renews a decades-old question: Is it beauty, or a blot?" *Star Tribune* (Minneapolis, MN), Jul. 19, 2008.

Albright, Thomas. "Sculpture That Touches on Extraordinary." *San Francisco Chronicle*, Sep. 2, 1982, p. 57.

_____. "Our Public Sculpture—A Disgrace?" *San Francisco Chronicle*, Aug. 21, 1983, Review section, pp. 11–12.

_____. "A Monumental Side of Arneson." *San Francisco Chronicle*, Feb. 22, 1984.

Alloway, Lawrence. "Chuck Ginnever: Space as a Continuum..." *Artforum*, Sep. 1967, pp. 36–39.

Amore, B. "Charles Ginnever." *Art New England*, vol. 38, no. 1, Jan./Feb. 2017, p. 16

Anderson, Wayne. "California Funk and the American Express." *Journal of Art*, vol. 4, no. 6, Jun./Jul./Aug. 1991, pp. 65–66.

Ashbery, John. "Telling it on the Mountain." *New York Magazine*, Aug. 27, 1979, p. 83.

Ayres, Jane. "Three Diverse Artists Showcase New Works in Garden." *Times Tribune*, Dec. 21, 1990, Lifestyles section.

Baker, Kenneth. "Chuck Ginnever." *Artforum*, Jan. 1972.

_____. (Review.) *Christian Science Monitor*, Dec. 20, 1971.

_____. "Sculpture That's Solid Paradox." *San Francisco Chronicle*, Jun. 24, 1986, p. 46

_____. "Esprit Sculpture Goes Public." *San Francisco Chronicle*, Sep. 1, 1987, p. 39.

_____. "Home-Grown Sculpture." *San Francisco Chronicle*, Mar. 31, 1988, p. E2.

_____. "In public art gets timid/With rare exceptions works on view in San Francisco tend to be cautious—or just mediocre." *San Francisco Chronicle*, Dec. 23, 2002.

_____. "Many ways to look at 'Rashomon'." *San Francisco Chronicle*, Nov. 25, 2012, Sunday Datebook, p. 37.

Batti, Renee. "The art of nature: Artists challenge Runnymede visitors to think anew about the space around them." *The Almanac* (Woodside, CA), Apr. 23, 2003.

Bell, David. "Beer, Parade, Flying Carnations Kick Off Art Show." *Albuquerque Journal*, Jul. 4, 1981.

_____. "400 Pieces on 13 Acres, 7th Shidoni Exhibition, Overwhelming, Exciting." *Albuquerque Journal*, Jul. 12, 1981, p. D-3.

_____. "Exhibits Challenge, Define Artworks as Objects." *Journal North*, Oct. 17, 1991.

Bissell, Therese. "The Art of Living Simply." *Architectural Digest*, May 2007, p. 280.

Braff, Phyllis. "Noted Works Highlight Sculpture Show." *New York Times*, Nov. 6, 1983.

Brenson, Michael. "The State of the City as Sculptors See It." *New York Times*, Jul. 27, 1990, pp. C1, C22.

Bry, Charlene. "Sculpture Seems to Change Its Shape Everytime You See It." *St. Louis Globe Democrat*, Jul. 7, 1982.

Burkhart, Dorothy. "Outward Appearances: Palo Alto Puts Its Art Where the Public Eye Is." *San Jose Mercury News*, Jun. 17, 1982, pp. 1D, 4D.

_____. "P.A. Show Follows Sculptural Tradition." *San Jose Mercury News*, Mar. 18, 1988, p. 17E.

Butterfield, Jan. "P.S.P.S., Project Sculpture/Public Sites." *Images & Issues*, vol. 3, no. 3, Nov./Dec. 1982, p. 49.

"Charles Ginnever's Rashomon and Amy Kaufman's drawings on view at San Jose Institute of Contemporary Art." *Artdaily.org*, Nov. 2012.

"Chauffered Scavenger Hunt Up For Bid at Woodside Auction." *Country Almanac* (Woodside, CA), May 10, 1989.

Cross, Miriam Dungan. "Trend in Bay Art Surveyed." *Oakland Tribune*, 1958.

Crossley, Mimi. "Lyrical Beams." *Houston Post*, Jun. 19, 1977.

Curtis, Cathy. "Galleries." *Los Angeles Times*, Oct. 23, 1987, part IV, pp. 20, 22.

Daley, Dave. "Art or Rusty Metal? Sculpture Debated." *Minneapolis Star*, Sep. 9, 1976.

Dietz, Betty A. "13 Sculptors in Panel Get Lost in Word Maze." *Dayton Daily News*, Mar. 9, 1977, p. 17.

Doss, Margaret Patterson. "An Ex-Military Hike." *San Francisco Chronicle*, Feb. 19, 1984, Sunday Punch section.

"Downtown Work of Art Goes Up." *Troy Daily News* (OH), 1980.

Ehrich, Lisa. "Splendors in the Grass." *Luxury Homes of the Metroplex* (Dallas), Spring 1984, pp. 52-60.

Ellenzweig, Allen. "Group Show." *Arts Magazine*, Apr. 1975, pp. 12–13.

Falaschi, Susan. "Sculptures Grow at Runnymede Farm." *Country Almanac*, vol. 23, no. 20, May 17, 1989.

Foote, Nancy. "Three Sculptors: Mark di Suvero, Richard Nonas, Chuck Ginnever." *Artforum*, no. 14, Feb. 1976, pp. 41-51.

Frantzis, Peggy. "Triton Adds 3 Works to Sculpture Garden." *Santa Clara Valley Weekly*, Jan. 3, 1991, p. 2.

"Gallery Hopping." *Pasatiempo* (Santa Fe), Oct. 18–24, 1991.

Gault, A. "Double Take: Sculptures Turning Japanese." *Santa Fe Reporter*, Sep. 28, 1988, p. 20.

Glueck, Grace. "Art: Isamu Noguchi and his world of stone." *New York Times*, May 21, 1983, Arts/Entertainment.

Goldshlack, Joey. "The largest piece of art in the University's collection: One big artistic statement." *Michigan Daily* (Ann Arbor, MI), Apr. 1, 2007.

Grant, Daniel. "Types of Insurance that Sculptors Regularly Need to Obtain for their Studios, Employees, and Exhibitions." *Sculpture Magazine*, vol. 24, no. 5, Jun. 2004.

Hurlburt, Roger. "Good Form." *Sun Sentinel*, Jan. 26, 1992.

Johnston, Theresa. "Don't just take it for granite: Outdoor art abounds on campus." *Stanford Report*, Jan. 28, 2004.

Kane, Karla. "Mountain View sculpture may cross the border." *Palo Alto Weekly*, Apr. 3, 2009.

Kay, Alfred. "Esprit Company Hosts Art Bay Area Exhibit." *Daily Report* (Ontario, CA), Jun. 8, 1987.

_____. "Esprit Headquarters Gets Into Spirit with Open-Air Art Exhibit." *Daily News* (Los Angeles, CA), Jun. 12, 1987.

_____. "Hi-tech Art Arises Amid the Warehouses." *Contra Costa Times*, Jun. 14, 1987.

Kelso, Jann. "Taking note..." *Dallas Morning News*, Apr. 3, 1984.

King, Mary. "New Sculpture at Laumeier." *St. Louis Post-Dispatcher*, Aug. 8, 1982.

Kleinfield, N. R. "8,000 New Battles at the 1040 Corral." *New York Times*, Mar. 13, 1988.

Kohen, Helen. "Art Looks for a Place in the Sun." *Artnews*, Feb. 1983, pp. 62–65.

Kozloff, Max. "The Further Adventures of American Sculpture." *Arts Magazine*, Feb. 1965, pp. 24–31.

Kramer, Hilton. "Month in Review." *Arts Magazine*, Nov. 1960, pp. 50–51.

Kroll, Jack. "Reviews and Previews: New Names This Month." *Artnews*, Dec. 1961, p. 21.

Kuspit, Donald B. "Authoritarian Abstraction." *The Journal of Aesthetics and Art Criticism*, vol. 36, no. 1, Autumn 1977, pp. 25–38.

Kutner, Janet. "Preview." *Dallas Morning News*, Mar. 16, 1984, Guide section, p. 3.

_____. "Landscape Geometrics—Sculptures Enliven Lee Park." *Dallas Morning News*, Jul. 10, 1984, pp. 1E–2E.

Lavin, Sylvia. "Power to Heal." *Elle Decor*, vol. 1, no. 5, Jun./Jul. 1990, pp. 80–89.

Lubell, Ellen. "Charles Ginnever." *Arts Magazine*, Jun. 1978, p. 45.

Masheck, Joseph. "Reviews." *Artforum*, Mar. 1973, p. 88.

McCaslin, Walt. "A Movin' Piece Any Way You Look At It." *Journal Herald* (Dayton, OH), Apr. 3, 1980.

McGill, Douglas C. "Nature Provides the Gallery For the Sculpture at Storm King." *New York Times*, May 31, 1985, pp. 11–12.

_____. "A Sculpture Gives Way to Petunias." *New York Times*, Oct. 23, 1986, p. 22.

McGovern, Judy. "Bells welcome new University of Michigan Museum of Art and its $41.9 million addition." *Ann Arbor News/mlive.com* (Ann Arbor, MI), Mar. 21, 2009.

McRae, Jacqueline. "Visions in Bronze." *Walla Walla Union-Bulletin* (WA), Nov. 17, 1988.

Meeker, Hubert. "Panel Explores Question of Sculpture's Survival." *Journal Herald* (Dayton, OH), Mar. 1966.

Megan, Kathy. "Field Narrowed for Post Office Sculptor." *Charleston Gazette* (WV), Nov. 22, 1979

Meline, Gabe. "Qualities of Belonging." *Bohemian* (Santa Rosa, CA), Feb. 20, 2008.

"Miami's Sculpture Drive-In." *USA Today*, Feb. 16, 1983, p. 4D.

"Minimalist/Abstract Sculptor, Charles Ginnever 'Rashomon' at San Jose Institute of Contemporary Art." *Artcentron.com*, Feb. 8, 2013.

Mintz, Howard. "13-ton Tribute to Dad." *Times Tribune* (Palo Alto, CA), Mar. 31, 1986, pp. A1, A10.

Morch, Al. "S/12: Sculpture Around the Bay." *San Francisco Examiner*, Aug. 4, 1982, p. E6.

Morris, Kenneth. "Rethinking Sculpture Conservation." *Sculpture*, vol. 6, no. 6, Nov./Dec. 1987, pp. 26–30.

"Museum Row, 'Les Funambules'." *Art and Architecture—San Francisco*, Jan. 12, 2012.

New York Arts Calendar, May/Jun. 1965.

"News Headlines." *New England Journal of Aesthetic Research*, May 8, 2008.

Nixon, Bruce. "A Question of Perspective: Sculpture by Charles Ginnever." *Sculpture Magazine,* vol. 2, no. 1, Jan./Feb. 2004.

"Outdoor Sculpture on View." *The Times* (San Mateo, CA), 1982, p. 25.

"Park Sculptures Generate Response!" *Oak Lawn Today* (Dallas, TX), vol. 4, no. 18, Apr. 12–25, 1984, pp. 1, 27.

Parker, Dian. "Steel Sculptures Amid Tendrils of Vine: The Legacy of Charles Ginnever." *Vermont Art Guide*, Issue #3, Winter 2017, pp. 24–30.

Parks, Louis B. "Sculpture Softens Downtown Vistas." *Houston Chroncle*, Feb. 19, 1981.

Pasatiempo (Santa Fe, NM), Oct. 18–24, 1991.

Patri, Tamara. "Hill Garden Opens Display." *Potrero View* (San Francisco), vol. 18, no. 5, Jun. 1987, p. 12.

Perry, Rebecca. "Art in the Park—Charles Ginnever's Sculpture Makes a Dynamic Open-air Exhibit." *Dallas Fort Worth Home & Garden*, Aug. 1984, pp. 50–54.

Peterson, Ivars. "Conference Report: ISAMA 2000." *Nexus Network Journal*, vol. 2 no. 4, Oct. 2000.

Peterson, William. "ConStruct at Shidoni's Sixth Annual Outdoor Sculpture Show." *Artspace*, Sep. 1980, pp. 54–58.

"Private Reserve." *Art-Talk* (CA), Dec. 1988.

Prospero, Ann Reaban. "Reviews: ConStruct South." *Art Papers*, Mar.–Apr. 1983, p. 24.

_____. "Sculpture: Monumental Efforts." *Miami/South Florida Magazine*, vol. 35, no. 7, May 1984, pp. 78–85.

Ratcliff, Carter. "New York Letter." *Art International*, vol. 19, no. 10, Dec. 20, 1975, p. 44.

_____. "Ginnever's *Daedalus*: Beyond Right-Angled Space." *Art in America*, May/Jun. 1976, pp. 98–100.

_____. "Taking Off: Four Sculptors and the Big New York Gesture." *Art in America*, Mar./Apr. 1978, pp. 106–107.

_____. "Charles Ginnever at Wooster Art Space." *Art in America*, Feb. 2005.

Raynor, Vivien. *New York Times*, May 30, 1980.

_____. "Sculpture Enhanced by a Dramatic Setting." *New York Times*, Aug. 23, 1981, p. 18.

_____. "Art: Explanations for 'Success of Failure'." *New York Times*, Dec. 21, 1984.

"Reviews and Previews." *Artnews*, 1967, p. 13.

Robins, Corinne. "Sculpture Now, 1974-1979." *Arts Magazine*, Nov. 1981, pp. 142–145.

Rose, Barbara. "A Harvest of Art at Andre's Sculpture Farm." *Journal of Art*, Oct. 1991, pp. 59–61.

Russell, John. "Art." *New York Times*, Nov. 4, 1977, p. C22.

_____. "Art." *New York Times*, Mar. 31, 1978.

_____. "When Art Came Out of the Studio and Mingled." *New York Times*, Oct. 1984, p. H33.

"Scale Model." *Charleston Gazette* (WV), Apr. 1980.

Schlinke, Britton. "Illusions of a Different Space." *Artweek* (CA), vol. 18, no. 25, Jul. 11, 1987, p. 6.

Shaw, Dan. "Site-Specific." *Interior Design*, Aug. 1, 2008.

Smith, Robert F. "Absolutely Abstract: Sculptor Charles Ginnever Finds Respect on a Grand Scale." *Rutland Daily Herald* (VT), Aug. 22, 1996, Vermonters section, p. 5.

"Sneak Preview of Upcoming Library Show." *Greenwich Times*, Nov. 26, 1971, p. 19.

Sykes, Jillus. "On the Grand Scale." *Sydney Morning Herald* (Australia), May 27, 1978, p. 15.

Taplin, Robert. "Tom Doyle and Lawrence Fane at Kouros—New York, New York." *Art in America*, Oct. 1999.

"The Choice of Sculpture is Yours." *Charleston Gazette* (WV), Mar. 19, 1980, pp. 1, 7.

"Three Prominent Bay Area Artists Make Long-term Loans to Triton Museum of Art." *Silicon Valley Visitors Guide* (CA), Jan. 1991.

"Today's Letters: 'Eyesores in Lee Park'; 'Beautiful Art in Lee Park.'" *Oak Lawn Today* (Dallas), Mar. 29, 1984, p. 17.

Van Proyen, Mark. "All the Young Cats." *Artweek*, vol. 22, no. 4, Jan. 31, 1991, pp. 1, 11.

Vidinghoff, Ed. "And You Thought Your Move Was Hard." *The New Mexican* (Santa Fe), Sep. 23, 1988, p. A3.

"Visual Arts." *Walla Walla Union Bulletin* (WA), Nov. 10, 1988, p. 14.

"Walking the Night Away: Second Summer Gallery Openings Friday." *Journal Newspapers*, (Ketchum, ID), Jul. 3, 1991, pp. 6B, 12B.

Weiss-Tisman, Howard. "Artist's Legacy Razed by Fire." *The Brattleboro Reformer* (VT), Aug. 21, 2003, pp. A1, A6.

Werner, Jessica. "120 acres of art: A tour of the private Runnymede Sculpture Farm." *Palo Alto Weekly,* May 19, 1995.

"Woodside Resident Knows What Mystery Object Is." *Times Tribune* (Palo Alto, CA), Aug. 10, 1987.

Yau, John. "The World According to Charles Ginnever." *Hyperallergic*, Jan. 13, 2013.

Graphite Drawing for Kitsune, 1993

SELECTED PUBLIC & PRIVATE COLLECTIONS

A

APEC Sculpture Garden, PICC, Manila, Philippines
Art Museum, Florida National University, Miami Beach, Florida
Australian National Gallery, Canberra, Australia

B

BankAmerica Corporation, Concord, California
The Bradley Foundation Sculpture Park, Milwaukee, Wisconsin

C

Cantor Arts Center, Stanford University, Stanford, California
City of Charleston/U.S. Post Office, Charleston, West Virginia
Chrysler Museum, Norfolk, Virginia
Clarinda Carnegie Art Museum, Clarinda, Iowa

D

Dayton Art Institute, Dayton, Ohio
Di Rosa Preserve, Napa, California
The Karen and Robert Duncan Collection, Lincoln, Nebraska

Steve Campbell, Jack Lemon, and Chuck Ginnever
working at Landfall Press, Santa Fe, NM, 2012

E

Edgewater Park, Cleveland Lakefront State Park, Cleveland, Ohio

G

General Mills, Inc., Minneapolis, Minnesota
General Services Administration, U.S. Courthouse, St. Paul, Minnesota
Grounds for Sculpture, Hamilton, New Jersey
Grove Isle Sculpture Garden, Coconut Grove, Florida

H

Hartwood Acres Park, Allegheny County, Pennsylvania
Herbert F. Johnson Museum of Art, Cornell University, Ithaca, New York
Hewlett Packard Corporation, Palo Alto, California
Hirshhorn Museum and Sculpture Garden, Washington, D.C.
Hobart School of Welding Technology, Troy, Ohio
Hughes Aircraft, Los Angeles, California
Hurd Development Corporation, Dallas, Texas

K

Knox Foundation, City of Houston, Texas
Koll-Bernal Associates, Pleasanton, California

L

Lake George Art Project, Lake George, New York
Laumeier International Sculpture Park, St. Louis, Missouri

M

Gayle Maxon-Edgerton Collection, Santa Fe, New Mexico
Metropolitan Museum of Art, New York, New York

N

Nathan Manilow Sculpture Park, Governor's State University, University Park, Illinois
National Museum of American Art, Smithsonian Institution, Washington, D.C.
Nelson Atkins Museum, Kansas City, Missouri
Neuberger Museum of Art, Purchase College, State University of New York, Purchase, New York
New Orleans Museum of Art, New Orleans, Louisiana

O

Orange County Museum of Art, Newport Beach, California

P

Park 470 Foundation, Chicago, Illinois
Park Central Hotel, San Francisco, California

R

City of Reno, Nevada
Runnymede Sculpture Farm, Woodside, California
JoAnn Sivley Ruppert Collection, Santa Fe, New Mexico

S

San Francisco Museum of Modern Art, San Francisco, California
City of San Mateo, California
Seattle Art Museum, Seattle, Washington
Sheldon Museum of Art, Lincoln, Nebraska
Shey Sculpture Collection, Gainesville, Florida
Stanford University Libraries, Department of Special Collections, Stanford, California
State University of New York, Albany, New York
State University of New York, Buffalo, New York
State University of New York, Purchase, New York
Storm King Art Center, Mountainville, New York
Sunrise Museum, Charleston, West Virginia

OPPOSITE
Green Mountain Blue II, 1978
National Gallery of Australia, Canberra

U

University of Houston, Houston, Texas
University of Michigan Museum of Art, Ann Arbor, Michigan

V

Virlane Foundation, New Orleans, Louisiana
Voigt Family Sculpture Foundation, Geyserville, California

W

Wadsworth Atheneum Museum of Art, Hartford, Connecticut
Walker Art Center, Minneapolis, Minnesota
City of Westport, Connecticut
City of Winston-Salem, North Carolina

ILLUSTRATIONS

FRONT AND BACK COVER
Origami Series III (1/4)
2012, Aluminum, acrylic lacquer
23 in. × 14 in. × 14 in. (variable)
58.4cm × 35.6cm × 35.6 cm (variable)
Photographer Unknown

p. ii
Chuck Ginnever working at Landfall Press,
Santa Fe, NM, 2012
Peter Ellzey, Photographer

p. iv
Ginnever works in progress at Landfall Press,
Santa Fe, NM, 2012
Peter Ellzey, Photographer

p. vi
Ginnever works in progress at Landfall Press,
Santa Fe, NM, 2012
Peter Ellzey, Photographer

p. viii
Zeus
1975, Steel, oil-based pigments
17 ft. × 45 ft. × 90 ft.
5.18m × 13.72m × 27.43m
Neil A. Lukas, Photographer

p. x
Sculptures from the Karen and
Robert Duncan Collection

ABOVE, LEFT/RIGHT
Louise Bourgeois (1911–2010)
Spider, 1996
Bronze and steel
Ricardo Barros, Photographer

Charles [Chuck] Ginnever
Rashomon (15 units), 1999
Steel
Barbara Emami, Photographer

CENTER, LEFT/RIGHT
Beverly Pepper (b. 1932)
Split Ritual, 1990
Cast iron
Ricardo Barros, Photographer

Levade (for Linda), 1978

Bernar Venet (b. 1941)
Arcs in Disorder: 22 Degrees Arc × 12, 2000
Rolled steel
Roger Bruhn, Photographer

Dennis Oppenheim (1938–2011)
Device to Root Out Evil, 2001
Aluminum, stainless steel,
fiberglass, blue glass
Ricardo Barros, Photographer

BELOW, LEFT/RIGHT
Richard Long (b. 1945)
Rain Line, 2005
Delabole steel
Ricardo Barros, Photographer

Magdalena Abakanowicz (1930–2017)
Untitled (from *Backs Series In 6 Parts*), 1988
Bronze
Ricardo Barros, Photographer

p. xi
Karen and Robert Duncan, 2017
Cole Sartore, Photographer

p. xii
Clarinda Carnegie Art Museum, Clarinda, Iowa
Alley Poyner Macchietto Architecture, Erin
Giannangelo, Photographer

p. xiv
ABOVE, LEFT/RIGHT
Interior views, Clarinda Carnegie Art Museum
Alley Poyner Macchietto Architecture, Erin
Giannangelo, Photographer

BELOW, LEFT/RIGHT
Students in CCAM educational programs
Sandra Williams, Photographer

p. xvi
Ithaca
1959, Wood, steel, mixed media
12 ft. × 25 ft. × 15 ft.
3.66m × 7.62m × 4.57m
Neil A. Lukas, Photographer

p. xviii
Oxbow (Cast 1/4) (two views)
1958; Cast 1989, Bronze with patina
80 in. × 36 in. × 18 in.
203.2cm × 91.4cm × 45.7cm
Karen and Robert Duncan Collection
M. Lee Fatherree, Photographer

p. xix
LEFT/RIGHT
Warp Series IV
1963, Stainless steel
24 in. × 30 in. × 24 in.
61.0cm × 76.2cm × 61.0cm
M. Lee Fatherree, Photographer

Warp Series V
1963, Stainless steel
24 in. × 30 in. × 24 in.
61.0cm × 76.2cm × 61.0cm
M. Lee Fatherree, Photographer

p. xx
ABOVE, LEFT/RIGHT
Détente Drawing I
1978, Graphite, ink wash on paper
8 in. × 8 in.
20.3cm × 20.3cm
M. Lee Fatherree, Photographer

Détente Drawing II
1978, Charcoal pencil on paper
11 in. × 7 in.
27.9cm × 17.8cm
M. Lee Fatherree, Photographer

Drawing of Four Sculptures
1979, Ink, graphite on paper
12 in. × 17.75 in.
30.5cm × 45.1cm
M. Lee Fatherree, Photographer

BELOW
Détente
1974, Steel
8.5 ft. × 6.5 ft. × 21 ft.
2.59m × 1.98m × 6.40m
Private Collection
Chuck Ginnever, Photographer

p. xxi
High Rise (two views)
1984, Steel
19 ft. × 22 ft. × 10 ft.
5.79m × 6.70m × 3.05m
Installation at Riverside Park, New York, NY
Chuck Ginnever, Photographer

p. xxii-xxiii
Didymous (three views)
1987, Steel
13.4 ft. × 21 ft. × 3.5 ft.
4.04m × 6.40m × 1.07m
Runnymede Sculpture Farm, Woodside, CA
M. Lee Fatherree, Photographer

p. xxiv
Godard's Dream (Maquette I) (two views)
1981, Steel, oil-based pigments
29 in. × 27.5 in. × 20 in.
73.7cm × 69.9cm × 50.8cm
John Nollendorfs, Photographer

p. xxv
Luna Moth Walk III, Luna Moth Walk II, Luna Moth Walk I
1982-85, Steel
Luna Moth Walk III: 14 ft. × 6 ft. × 7 ft.;
4.26m × 1.83m × 2.13m
Luna Moth Walk II: 8.5 ft. × 6.25 ft. × 10.25 ft.;
2.59m × 1.91m × 3.12m
Luna Moth Walk I: 9.5 ft. × 8 ft. × 7.5 ft.;
2.90m × 2.44m × 2.29m
Clarinda Carnegie Art Museum, Clarinda, IA
M. Lee Fatherree, Photographer

p. xxvi
ABOVE, LEFT/RIGHT
Aerial Drawing Series No. 7
1995, Mixed media on paper
5.5 in. × 8.5 in.
14.0cm × 21.6cm
M. Lee Fatherree, Photographer

Aerial Drawing Series No. 11
2000, Mixed media on paper
5.5 in. × 8.5 in.
14.0cm × 21.6cm
M. Lee Fatherree, Photographer

BELOW, LEFT/RIGHT
Aerial Drawing Series No. 15
2000, Mixed media on paper
5.5 in. × 8.5 in.
14.0cm × 21.6cm
M. Lee Fatherree, Photographer

Aerial Drawing Series No. 12
2000, Mixed media on paper
5.5 in. × 8.5 in.
14.0cm × 21.6cm
M. Lee Fatherree, Photographer

p. xxvii
LEFT
Atlantis Drawing V
1978, Ink, crayon on paper
18.75 in. × 23.9 in.
47.6cm × 60.6cm
M. Lee Fatherree, Photographer

RIGHT, ABOVE/BELOW
Atlantis
1976, Steel
10 ft. × 36 ft. × 36 ft.
3.05m × 10.97m × 10.97m
State University of New York, Buffalo, NY
Photographer Unknown

Atlantis (Maquette)
1976, Steel
9 in. × 25 in. × 27 in.
22.9cm × 63.5cm × 68.6cm
M. Lee Fatherree, Photographer

p. xxviii
Rashomon (15 units)
1999, Steel
Each: 42 in. × 42 in. × 42 in.
Each: 106.7cm × 106.7cm × 106.7cm
Karen and Robert Duncan Collection
Carl Sartore, Photographer

p. xxix
Rashomon (15 units)
1999, Steel
Each: 42 in. × 42 in. × 42 in.
Each: 106.7cm × 106.7cm × 106.7cm
Karen and Robert Duncan Collection
John Nollendorfs, Photographer

p. xxx
Rashomon Etching – Nine Positions
1994, Etching: Printer's ink on paper
Image: 17.75 in. × 17.6 in.; 45.1cm × 44.8cm
Sheet: 29.75 in. × 22 in.; 75.6cm × 55.9cm
M. Lee Fatherree, Photographer

p. xxxi
Rashomon (3 Units)
1998, Steel
Each: 13 ft. × 13 ft. × 13 ft.
Each: 3.96m × 3.96m × 3.96m
Private Collection
M. Lee Fatherree, Photographer

p. xxxii
Nautilus
1976, Cor-ten steel
11 ft. × 22 ft. × 34 ft. (variable)
3.35m × 6.71m × 10.36m (variable)
Collection Walker Art Center, Minneapolis, MN
Acquired with funds from Dr. and Mrs. John S. Jacoby in memory of John Dixon Jacoby; Suzanne Walker and Thomas N. Gilmore; the Art Center Acquisition Fund; and the National Endowment for the Arts, 1976 (1976.17)
Photograph Courtesy of Walker Art Center

INFINITE FOLD: GINNEVER'S EXPRESSIVE GEOMETRY

1. *Godard's Dream*
1982, Aluminum, acrylic-polymer paint
14 ft. × 15 ft. × 11 ft.
4.26m × 4.57m × 3.35m
Robert E. Mates, Photographer

2-3. *Nike* (two views)
1986, Bronze with patina
8 ft. × 9.8 ft. × 6.7 ft.
2.67m × 3.05m × 2.03m
APEC Sculpture Garden, PICC, Manila,
Philippines
M. Lee Fatherree, Photographer

4. Gian Lorenzo Bernini (1598–1680)
*L'Estasi di Santa Teresa (The Ecstasy of St.
Theresa)*
1647–52, Marble
Cornaro Chapel, Santa Maria della Vittoria, Rome
SCALA / Art Resource, NY

5. *Luna Moth Walk III*
1982, Steel
14 ft. × 6 ft. × 7 ft.
4.27m × 1.83m × 2.13m
Clarinda Carnegie Art Museum
John Nollendorfs, Photographer

6. *Luna Moth Walk I*
1982, Steel
9.5 ft. × 8 ft. × 7.5 ft.
2.90m × 2.44m × 2.29m
Clarinda Carnegie Art Museum
John Nollendorfs, Photographer

7. *Luna Moth Walk II*
1985, Steel
8.5 ft. × 6.25 ft. × 10.25 ft.
2.59m × 1.91m × 3.12m
Clarinda Carnegie Art Museum
Cole Sartore, Photographer

8-9. *Luna Moth Walk I Maquette* (two views)
1981, Steel, oil-based pigments
26 in. × 24 in. × 19 in.
66.0cm × 60.9cm × 48.3cm
John Nollendrofs, Photographer

10. Antony Gormley (b. 1950)
Vessel
2012, Cor-ten steel, M16 countersunk steel
screws
12.1 ft. × 72.2 ft. × 15.75 ft.
3.70m × 22.0m × 4.80m
Installation view, Galleria Continua, San
Gimignano, Italy, 2012
Photograph by Ela Bialkowska, OKNO STUDIO,
Courtesy of Galleria Continua, © the artist

11. Xavier Veilhan (b. 1963)
Laurence
2014, Aluminum, polyurethane paint, birchwood
70.9 in. *x* 10.1 in. × 9.4 in.
180.0cm × 25.6cm × 24.0cm
Collection Fundación AMMA
© 2018 Veilhan ADAGP, Paris / ARS, New York
Photograph © Diane Arques

12-14.
San Mateo Bridge
1978, Steel
9 ft. × 25 ft. × 8 ft.
2.74m × 7.62m × 2.44m
City of San Mateo, California
M. Lee Fatherree, Photographer

15. *Bop and Crazed*
1980, Steel, oil-based pigments
John Nollendorfs, Photographer

16. *Bop*
1980, Steel, oil-based pigments
5.2 ft. × 4 ft. × 4.5 ft.
1.57m × 1.22m × 1.37m
M. Lee Fatherree, Photographer

17. *Crazed*
1980, Steel, oil-based pigments
3.75 ft. × 5.25 ft. × 5.2 ft.
1.14m × 1.60m × 1.57m
M. Lee Fatherree, Photographer

18-20. *Bop and Crazed*
1980, Steel, oil-based pigments
John Nollendorfs, Photographer

21-22. *Chicago Triangles* (two views)
1979, Steel
7 ft. × 24 ft. × 5 ft.
2.13m × 7.32m × 1.52m
Iris & B. Gerald Cantor Center for Visual Arts,
Stanford University, Stanford, CA
Given in honor of Gerhard Casper, President,
Stanford University (1992–2000), by Mr. and Mrs.
Milo Gates (2000.43)
M. Lee Fatherree, Photographer

23-25. *No Place to Hide* (three views)
1986, Steel
20 ft. × 45 ft. × 30 ft.
6.09m × 13.72m × 9.14m
Cole Sartorre, Photographer

26. *Rashomon* (15 units)
1999, Steel
Each: 42 in. × 42 in. × 42 in.
Each: 106.7cm × 106.7cm × 106.7cm
Karen and Robert Duncan Collection
Cole Sartorre, Photographer

27. *Rashomon Sculpture Study IV – Four Positions*
1993, Ink, ink wash on paper
10.9 in. × 13.9 in.
27.7cm × 35.3cm
M. Lee Fatherree, Photographer

28. *Rashomon (Table with 11 Maquettes)*
1994, Bronze with patina
4.2 ft. × 7 ft. × 1.4 ft.
1.27m × 2.13m × 0.43m
Gayle Maxon-Edgerton Collection
M. Lee Fatherree, Photographer

29. *Rashomon* (Deluxe copy with maquette)
2014, Limited-edition artists' book with
etchings and letterpress printing
16.1 in. × 12 in. × 1.75 in.
41.0cm × 30.5cm × 4.4cm
James Hart, Photographer

30. *Rashomon X*
1994, Bronze with patina
Each: 9 in. × 10 in. × 11 in. (variable)
Each: 22.9cm × 25.4cm × 27.9cm (variable)
M. Lee Fatherree, Photographer

31. *Rashomon* (15 units), 1999,
installed at San Jose Institute for Contemporary
Art, 2012
M. Lee Fatherree, Photographer

32. *Calligraphic Sculpture*
1958, Wood, steel
9 ft. × 10 ft. × 2 ft.
2.74m × 3.05m × 0.61m
Chuck Ginnever, Photographer

33. *Ithaca*
1959, Wood, steel, mixed media
12 ft. × 25 ft. × 15 ft.
3.66m × 7.62m × 4.57m
Chuck Ginnever, Photographer

34. *Calligraphic Sculpture, 1958 (Working Drawing No. 1)*
1958, Graphite on paper
10.5 in. × 8 in.
26.7cm × 20.3cm
M. Lee Fatherree, Photographer

35-36. Tom Doyle (left) and Charles Ginnever
(right) in Sculpture Dance, *Ergo Suits Carnival*,
1962
Skip Mason, Photographer, from 16mm film

37-38. *Jezabel* (two views)
1964, Steel, wood, chromed steel
44 in. × 54 in. × 44 in.
111.8cm × 137.2cm × 111.8cm
M. Lee Fatherree, Photographer

39-40. *Steel Maquette with Mirror II* (two views)
1963, Steel, oil-based enamel, mirror
6 in. × 12 in. × 12 in.
15.2cm × 30.5cm × 30.5cm
Private Collection
M. Lee Fatherree, Photographer

41-42. *Timebridge* (two views)
1964, Steel, oil-based enamel
15 in. × 29 in. × 25 in.
38.1cm × 73.7cm × 63.5cm
Private Collection
M. Lee Fatherree, Photographer

43. *Dante's Rig*
1964, Aluminum, steel, oil-based pigments
13 ft. × 15 ft. × 25 ft.
3.96m × 4.57m × 7.62m
Neil A. Lukas, Photographer

44. *Midas and Fog*
1966, Steel, acrylic lacquer
7 ft. × 18 ft. × 6 ft.
2.13m × 5.49m × 1.83m
Private Collection
Photographer Unknown

45. *3 + 1*
1967, Cor-ten steel
4 ft. × 14 ft. × 3 ft.
1.22m × 4.27m × 0.91m
The Metropolitan Museum of Art, New York
Gift of Ellen and Peter Rosenau, 1983 (1983.613)
Chuck Ginnever, Photographer

46. Untitled (Flat Illusion, for Joseph H. Hirshhorn II)
1968, Cor-ten steel
A: 4.25 ft. × 8.8 ft. × 1.5 ft.
1.29m × 2.69m × .43m
B: 4.8 ft. × 8 ft. × 4.7 ft.
1.48m × 2.44m × 1.42m
Hirshhorn Museum and Sculpture Garden, Washington, DC
Gift of Joseph H. Hirshhorn, 1972 (72.134)
Photographer Unknown

47. *High Rise*, 1984, and *Medusa*, 1986, installed at Riverside Park, New York, October 2014
Ronnie Ginnever, Photographer

48. *High Rise*
1984, Steel
19 ft. × 22 ft. × 10 ft.
5.79m × 6.71m × 3.05m
Chuck Ginnever, Photographer

49. *Medusa*
1986, Steel
12 ft. × 38 ft. × 32 ft.
3.66m × 11.58m × 9.75m
M. Lee Fatherree, Photographer

50-51. *Dementia* (two views)
1998, Steel
8.7 ft. × 16 ft. × 6 ft.
2.64m × 4.88m × 1.83m
John Nollendorfs, Photographer

52-53. *Azuma* (two views)
1987, Bronze with patina
10.5 ft. × 5.75 ft. × 8.5 ft.
3.20m × 1.75m × 2.59m
Tara J Graves, Photographer

54-57. *Moonwalker I* (four views)
1989, Bronze with patina
17 in. × 17 in. × 8 in.
43.2cm × 43.2cm × 20.3cm
M. Lee Fatherree, Photographer

58-59. *Origami Series III* (Unique) (two views)
2012, Aluminum, acrylic lacquer
11 in. × 6.5 in. × 5.5 in. (variable)
27.9cm × 16.5cm × 14.0cm (variable)
M. Lee Fatherree, Photographer

60-61. *Origami Series Maquettes* (two views)
Chuck Ginnever, Photographer

62-63. *Origami Series I* (Unique) (two views)
2012, Aluminum, acrylic lacquer
11 in. × 5.25 in. × 4 in. (variable)
27.9cm × 13.3cm × 10.2cm (variable)
M. Lee Fatherree, Photographer

64-67. *Origami Series II* (A/P) (four views)
2012, Aluminum, acrylic lacquer
11.5 in. × 7.75 in. × 6 in. (variable)
29.2cm × 19.7cm × 15.2cm (variable)
M. Lee Fatherree, Photographer

DAEDALUS

68-69. *Daedalus*
1975, Steel
10.7 ft. × 30 ft. × 21 ft.
3.25m × 9.14m × 6.40m
University of Michigan Museum of Art, Ann Arbor, MI
Acquired with funds from the Thirtieth Anniversary Project and the National Endowment for the Arts
Patrick Young, Michigan Imaging

70. *Atlantis*
1976, Steel
10 ft. × 36 ft. × 36 ft.
3.05m × 10.97m × 10.97m
State University of New York, Buffalo, NY
Photographer Unknown

71. *Olympus*
1976, Steel
13 ft. × 32 ft. × 32 ft.
3.35m × 9.75m × 9.75m
The Bradley Foundation, Milwaukee, WI
Photographer Unknown

72-73. *Crete*
1976–78, Cor-ten steel
53.1 ft. × 16.3 ft. × 11.6 ft.
16.18m × 4.98m × 3.53m
Laumeier Sculpture Park Collection, St. Louis, MO
Gift of Adam and Judy Aronson
Photographer Unknown

74. *Protagoras*
1976, Steel
10 ft. × 30 ft. × 14 ft.
3.05m × 9.14m × 4.27m
U.S. General Services Administration, Burger Federal Building, St. Paul, MN
Photographer Unknown

75-77. *Troika II*
2003, Steel
8 ft. × 14 ft. × 4 ft.
2.44m × 4.27m × 1.22m
JoAnn Sivley Ruppert Collection, NM
Gayle Maxon-Edgerton, Photographer

78-84. *Daedalus*
1975, Steel
10.7 ft. × 30 ft. × 21 ft.
3.25m × 9.14m × 6.40m
University of Michigan Museum of Art,
Ann Arbor, MI
Acquired with funds from the Thirtieth
Anniversary Project and the
National Endowment for the Arts
Patrick Young, Michigan Imaging

RASHOMON

85. *Rashomon* (15 units), 1999,
Iowa State University, Ames, 2014
Chuck Ginnever: Rashomon was a collaboration
of the Center for Contemporary Art, Santa Fe,
NM, and Chuck Ginnever in association with
Gayle Maxon-Edgerton, GME LLC, Santa Fe, NM.
Installed in the Food Sciences Courtyard, Iowa
State University, November 24, 2014–July 1,
2015.
Photograph courtesy of University Museums,
Iowa State University, Ames

86. Poster for Robert Wiene's 1920 silent film
*The Cabinet of Dr. Caligari (Das Cabinet des Dr.
Caligari)*
World History Archive / Alamy Stock Photo

87. Film still from Robert Wiene's *The Cabinet
of Dr. Caligari*, German silent film, 1920
World History Archive / Alamy Stock Photo

88-89. Two scenes from Akira Kurosawa's 1950
film, *Rashomon*
INTERFOTO / Alamy Stock Photo

90. Poster for Kurosawa's *Rashomon*
TOHO COMPANY / Ronald Grant Archive /
Alamy Stock Photo

91. *Rashomon* (15 units), 1999,
installed at San Jose Institute for Contemporary
Art, 2012
M. Lee Fatherree, Photographer

92. *Gyro I*
1982, Steel
12.2 ft. × 29 ft. × 19.25 ft.
3.71m × 8.84m × 5.87m
John Nollendorfs, Photographer

93-94. *Hangover II* (two views)
1983, Steel
13 ft. × 37 ft. × 7 ft.
3.96m × 11.28m × 2.13m
M. Lee Fatherree, Photographer

95. *Rashomon* (3 units)
1995, Bronze with patina
5 ft. × 5 ft. × 5 ft. (variable)
1.52m × 1.52m × 1.52m (variable)
Di Rosa Preserve, Napa, CA
M. Lee Fatherree, Photographer

96. *Rashomon Sculpture Study V*
1994, Ink, ink wash on paper
13.9 in. × 10.9 in.
35.3cm × 27.7cm
M. Lee Fatherree, Photographer

97-108. *Rashomon* (15/40)
2014, Limited-edition artists' book with
etchings and letterpress printing
12.25 in. × 16.25 in. × 1.5 in.
31.1cm × 41.3cm × 3.8cm
Karen and Robert Duncan Collection
M. Lee Fatherree, Photographer

109. *Rashomon Etching – Position 8*
1994, Intaglio etching: Printer's ink on paper
3.9 in. × 5.9 in.
9.9cm × 15.0cm
M. Lee Fatherree, Photographer

110. *Rashomon Etching – Six Positions*
1994, Intaglio: Printer's ink on paper
Image: 17.9 in. × 17.75 in.; 45.4cm × 45.1cm
Sheet: 29.75 in. × 22.1 in.; 75.6cm × 56.2cm
M. Lee Fatherree, Photographer

111. *Rashomon Sculpture Study VI – Six Positions*
1995, Ink, ink wash on paper
10.9 in. × 13.9 in.
27.7cm × 35.3cm
M. Lee Fatherree, Photographer

MULTUS

112. *Multus*, 2012
2012, Folded sculpture: Three-color lithograph
on 500g, 3-ply Sommerset paper
12 in. × 20 in. × 18 in.
30.5cm × 50.8cm × 45.7cm
Printed in an edition of 20 by Landfall Press,
Santa Fe, NM
Peter Ellzey, Photographer

113. *Multus* (Maquette), 2012
Peter Ellzey, Photographer

114. *Multus* (Sheet), 2012
2012, Folded sculpture: Three-color lithograph
on 500g, 3-ply Sommerset paper
20 in. × 18 in.
50.8cm × 45.7cm
Printed in an edition of 20 by Landfall Press,
Santa Fe, NM
M. Lee Fatherree, Photographer

115. Instructions for folding *Multus*
M. Lee Fatherree, Photographer

116-120. *Multus*, 2012 (five views)
2012, Folded sculpture: Three-color lithograph
on 500g, 3-ply Sommerset paper
12 in. × 20 in. × 18 in.
30.5cm × 50.8cm × 45.7cm
Printed in an edition of 20 by Landfall Press,
Santa Fe, NM
M. Lee Fatherree, Photographer

p. 68
Mirage
2005, Steel
17 ft. × 17 ft. × 17 ft.
5.18m × 5.18m × 5.18m
Brenden Hussey, Photographer

p. 70
Chuck Ginnever working at Landfall Press, Santa
Fe, NM, 2012
Peter Ellzey, Photographer

p. 77
Installation view, *Charles Ginnever: Rashomon*,
San Jose Institute of Contemporary Art,
San Jose, CA, 2012
M. Lee Fatherree, Photographer

p. 78
Chuck Ginnever at Landfall Press with
Jack Lemon and Steve Campbell, 2012
Peter Ellzey, Photographer

p. 81
Catalogues of Chuck Ginnever's work
M. Lee Fatherree, Photographer

p. 85
Graphite Drawing for Kitsune
1993, Graphite on paper
5 in. × 8 in.
12.7cm × 20.3cm
M. Lee Fatherree, Photographer

p. 86
Steve Campbell, Jack Lemon, and Chuck
Ginnever working at Landfall Press, Santa Fe, NM,
2012
Peter Ellzey, Photographer

p. 89
Green Mountain Blue II
1978, Steel, steel cable, oil-based pigments
26.2 ft. × 69.9 ft. × 3.9 ft.
8.00m × 21.30m × 1.20m
National Gallery of Australia, Canberra
Gift of John Kahlbetzer 1981 (NGA 81.3072)
Photographer Unknown

p. 90
Levade (for Linda)
1978, Steel
16 ft. × 40 ft. × 30 ft.
4.88m × 12.19m × 9.14m
Eric Sutherland, Photographer

p. 99
Charles Ginnever Maquettes (Travelling Case)
Created for Chuck Ginnever by Jonathan Berger
and Brenden Hussey
Brendan Hussey, Photographer

p. 100
Gyro I
1982, Steel
12.2 ft. × 29 ft. × 19.25 ft.
3.71m × 8.84m × 5.87m
Cole Sartore, Photographer

98

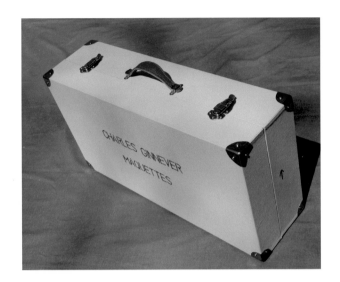

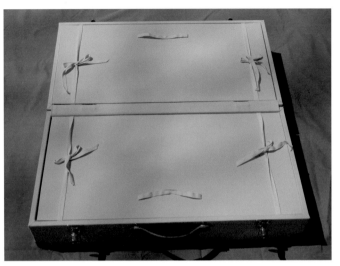

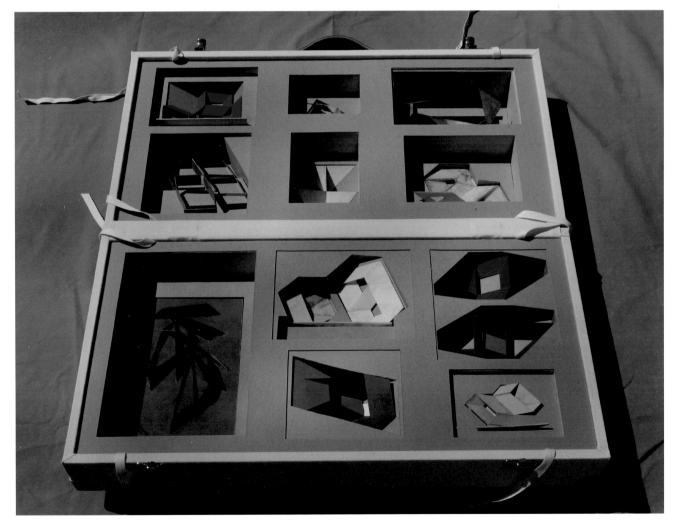

Charles Ginnever Maquettes
(Travelling Case)
Created for Chuck Ginnever
by Jonathan Berger and
Brenden Hussey

99

ACKNOWLEDGMENTS

A PROJECT OF THIS SCOPE requires the coordination, skills, and dedication of a sizeable team. Thus, a debt of gratitude is due every individual involved in the publication of this catalogue, the organization of the Clarinda Carnegie Art Museum exhibition, *Charles [Chuck] Ginnever: Folded Forms*, and the installation of more than a dozen of Ginnever's sculptures at outdoor sites in Clarinda, Iowa, and Lincoln, Nebraska.

Primarily, we would like to thank Chuck Ginnever, whose extraordinary ability to see the world from countless points of view has made this project possible. He has generously given his talent, time, and expertise to bring the exhibition to fruition, offering Midwestern audiences the opportunity to share his unique vision for years to come.

We would like to acknowledge Gayle Maxon-Edgerton, GME LLC, who is Ginnever's representative and long-time supporter of his ideas and his work. Without her, the exhibition would not have happened.

It is a privilege for Iowans and Nebraskans to have access to these historically significant works. Thankfully, this catalogue will carry that pleasure to an even larger audience. We are indebted to David Ebony and John Yau for their insightful essays on Ginnever's work as well as A. Bret Waller's 1977 essay; the excellent photography provided by M. Lee Fatherree, John Nollendorfs, Cole Sartore, Peter Ellzey, Brenden

Gyro I, 1982

101

Hussey, James Hart, Roger Bruhn, Erin Giannangelo, Ricardo Barros, Barbara Emami, and others; the design and layout of the catalogue by John Hubbard/ EMKS, Finland; Anne Kohs & Associates for coordinating the design, layout, photography, and production of the catalogue; Diane Roby for securing permissions for photography, assembling the artist's biography, bibliography, and collections, as well as her editorial efforts on the authors' behalf; Pam Rino Evans, who organized and coordinated the photography for the catalogue; Gary Hawkey, John Bailey, and Stephanie Lock, at iocolor, LLP, Seattle, for their expert color management and coordination of the catalogue; and for the professional, high-quality printing and binding of this publication by Artron Color Printing Company, China.

Steve Jensen has, again, capably overseen the installation of each interior and exterior work, while Cross and Sons Transport of Seward, Nebraska, assured that each sculpture was properly loaded and delivered in excellent condition.

We thank the Mayors and City Councils of Clarinda and Lincoln, as well as the Lincoln Parks and Recreation Department staff, who supported the endeavor and conscientiously assured attractive and appropriate sites in their communities for Ginnever's sculptures.

We wish to acknowledge Clarinda Carnegie Art Museum founders Karen and Robert Duncan for graciously continuing to share their art, hearts, and resources. Their enthusiastic support of all aspects of the Ginnever project advances their goal of making art an accessible part of our community experience.

The role of CCAM Director Trish Bergren deserves special recognition. She has worked tirelessly to coordinate the placement and installation of the works in Clarinda and has developed first-rate educational programming related to the sculptural installations as well as the museum exhibition.

Finally, the value of CCAM docents and junior docents—their curiosity, enthusiasm, and willingness to get every job done—keeps the staff motivated and eager to get up in the morning.

Anne Pagel, Curator

I WOULD LIKE TO ACKNOWLEDGE a number of family members, associates, and friends who have supported my work over the many years I have made sculpture, including my parents, Helyne and Charles Ginnever; my daughters, Jodi and Chloe, and their mothers Ronnie and Susan.

I appreciate those who have helped me fabricate my sculptures, such as David Rohn, Frank Sansone, Tom Greer, Mark Goodenaux, Matt Gil, Johnny Swing, and Michael Ben. I extend my appreciation to Mark Anderson and the craftsmen at Walla Walla Foundry, and to Brattleboro Sheet Metal, Ted Moser, Picture Car Warehouse.

I want to acknowledge Louise Newquist, who rescued me after the devastating studio fire that destroyed much of my work and files; Mark di Suvero, who allowed me to use his Petaluma studio after the fire, and who has been a friend and advocate for my work; and Susie Schlesinger, who let me install sculptures on her land.

Recognition is due to Muna Tsang Dance Group, who choreographed a dance performance based on my sculpture installation at Riverside Park, New York; Kevin Hearle, who was so helpful with the placement of *San Mateo Bridge* in my hometown of San Mateo, California; Cathy Kimball, Executive Director, San Jose Institute of Contemporary Art; Lynette Pohlman, Director, Iowa State University Museums; Al and Judy Voigt, Voigt Family Foundation; and to MJ Klimenko for years of moral support and encouragement.

I want to thank Neil A. Lukas and M. Lee Fatheree, who have photographed my work for many years; Debby Lazar, who processes my photographs; George Ladas, who designed my website; and Jonathan Berger and Brendon Hussey, who for several years worked on preparing a video to document my work and ideas. I'm grateful to Jack Lemon and Steve Campbell at Landfall Press, who printed the etchings for the *Rashomon* artists' book and accepted the challenge of turning 2-dimensional cardboard into a 3-dimensional sculpture edition. Peggy Gotthold and Lawrence Van Velzer at Foolscap Press translated my ideas about multiple views of an object into the design, printing, and binding of the *Rashomon* artists' book.

Finally, I thank Anne Kohs, Gayle Maxon-Edgerton, Anne Pagel, and Karen and Robert Duncan for their vision and unwavering support of my work and ideas.

Chuck Ginnever

GINNEVER

This catalogue is published in conjunction with the exhibition *Charles [Chuck] Ginnever: Folded Forms*, organized by the Clarinda Carnegie Art Museum, Clarinda, Iowa, June 24–December 4, 2018.

Commissions and sales of Charles Ginnever's works are through Gayle Maxon-Edgerton, Santa Fe, NM.

Copyright of artworks by Charles Ginnever is held by the artist. Text copyrights published in the catalogue are held by their respective authors. Photography copyrights are held by their respective photographers.

Photography credits:

Diane Arques, Page 6 (Illus. No. 11); **Ricardo Barros**, Page x (all photographs except above right and center); **Ela Bialkowska**/OKNO Studio, Page 6 (Illus. No. 10); **Roger Bruhn**, Page x (center); **Peter Ellzey**, Pages ii, iv, vi, 62 (Illus. No. 112), 64 (Illus. No. 113), 70, 78, 86; **Barbara Emami**, Page x (above right); **M. Lee Fatherree**, Pages xviii, xix, xx (above), xxii-xxiii, xxv, xxvi, xxvii (left and below right), xxx, xxxi, 3 (Illus. No. 2-3), 6–7 (Illus. No. 12-14), 8 (Illus. No. 16), 9 (Illus. No. 17), 10 (Illus. No. 21-22), 13–14, 16–17, 18 (Illus. No. 34), 20, 25, 28-30, 31 (Illus. No. 62-63), 32, 51 (Illus. No. 91), 53–61, 64 (Illus. No. 114), 65–67, 77, 81, 85; **Erin Giannangelo**/Alley Poyner Macchietto Architecture, Pages xii, xiv; **Chuck Ginnever**, Pages xx (below), xxi, 18 (Illus. No. 32-33), 22 (Illus. No. 45), 24 (Illus. No. 48), 31 (Illus. No. 60-61); **Ronnie Ginnever**, Page 24 (Illus. No. 47); **Tara J Graves**, Page 27; **James Hart**, Page 15; **Brenden Hussey**, Pages 68, 99; **Neil A. Lukas**, Pages viii, xvi, 21; **Skip Mason**, Page 19; **Gayle Maxon-Edgerton**, Page 40; **Robert E. Mates**, Page 2; **John Nollendorfs**, Pages xxiv, xxix, 4 (Illus. No. 5-6), 5, 8 (Illus. No. 15), 9 (Illus. No. 18-20), 26, 52; **Cole Sartore**, Pages xi, xxviii, 4 (Illus. No. 7), 11–12, 100; **Eric Sutherland**, Page 90; University Museums, Iowa State University, Ames, Iowa, Page 48; Walker Art Center, Minneapolis, Page xxxii; **Sandra Williams,** Page xiv (below); **Patrick Young/Michigan Imaging**, Pages 34, 36, 41–47.

Special thanks for photography and assistance to: INTERFOTO/Alamy Stock Photo, Page 51 (Illus. No. 88-89); SCALA/Art Resource, NY, Page 3 (Illus. No. 4); TOHO COMPANY/Ronald Grant Archive/Alamy Stock Photo, Page 51 (Illus. No. 90); World History Archive/Alamy Stock Photo, Page 50; Bea Bradley, White Cube; Joyce Faust, Art Resource NY; Kayla Hagen, Walker Art Center; Cathy Kimball, San Jose Institute for Contemporary Art; Caroline Riehl, Atelier Xavier Veilhan; Allison Sheridan, University Museums, Iowa State University, Ames.

Copyright for this publication is held by Anne Kohs & Associates, Inc., 2018.

All rights reserved under International and Pan-American Copyright Conventions. No part of this publication may be reproduced or transmitted in any form or by any means, electronic or mechanical, including photocopy, recording or any other information storage and retrieval system, or otherwise without written permission from Anne Kohs & Associates, Inc.

Library of Congress Control Number: 2018944705

ISBN: 978-0-692-12716-2

Catalogue concept, research, and project coordination by Anne Kohs & Associates, Inc., Portola Valley, California. www.artistsforum.com

Edited by Pam Rino Evans, Anne Pagel, and Diane Roby. Image management by Pam Rino Evans.

Designed by John Hubbard / EMKS, Finland

Typeset in Gill Sans Light by EMKS, Finland

Color and print management by iocolor, LLP, Seattle, Washington

Printed and bound by Artron Color Printing Company, China

"One of the most significant and little-celebrated innovations in late 20th century art: Charles Ginnever's 'Rashomon' suite. ... Much important sculpture of our era has concerned itself with tensions between the bodily and mental grasp of the real. 'Rashomon' goes to the heart of that matter, defying its viewers to compare its identical components by rotating them mentally."
— Kenneth Baker, *San Francisco Chronicle*, 2012

"Mysteries of perception have always been an issue with Chuck and he was one of the first artists to probe the nature of spatial experience using predominately abstract forms. Carter Ratcliff states that in his work, Ginnever is attempting to shift responsibility for the experience of the work away from the kinds of cultural determinations embedded in Western spatial systems. Ginnever's sculptures will always be different, for each viewer, each time they are seen. Years later Ratcliff described the ability of Chuck's work to reach beyond its own space, thus encouraging the eye to consider space itself as a flexible, inherently unstable medium in its own right.

Chuck has always brought certain concerns of his own—his mysteries of perception—to wide open sculptural environments. His works are of intense visual delight and they are decidedly peripatetic. Ginnever is quite skilled at playing against our visual habit—where the eye expects gravity to exert itself, the work springs into space, and as the spectator moves around it, a reading of material weight is challenged as the forms seem to disappear, as though suddenly weightless."
— Carter Ratcliff, summarized from Bruce Nixon
in *Sculpture Magazine*, Jan./Feb. 2004

"Charles Ginnever has been under-appreciated by critics, but he is an artist who has created a unique body of work that pulls us toward a visceral understanding of the nature of visual perception. Rooted in Japanese and Eastern teachings, Ginnever constructs large scale sculptures that must be experienced in situ. As the viewer moves around one of his elegant yet powerful metal constructions the landscape becomes the 'other element' in the work. A variety of vistas are framed while the form of the sculpture itself morphs Rashomon-like into different shapes—thereby underscoring the subjective nature of the way we see. Ginnever's multi-positional, interactive work plays against complacent visual tendencies, as the artist has noted, using traditional means to challenge atrophied habits of perception."
— Deborah Rothschild, Ph.D., Senior Curator Emerita,
Williams College Museum of Art, 2014

"One of the most significant and little-celebrated innovations in late 20th century art: Charles Ginnever's 'Rashomon' suite. ... Much important sculpture of our era has concerned itself with tensions between the bodily and mental grasp of the real. 'Rashomon' goes to the heart of that matter, defying its viewers to compare its identical components by rotating them mentally."

— Kenneth Baker, San Francisco Chronicle, 2012

"Mysteries of perception have always been an issue with Chuck and he was one of the first artists to probe the nature of spatial experience using predominately abstract forms. Carter Ratcliff states that in his work, Ginnever is attempting to shift responsibility for the experience of the work away from the kinds of cultural determinations embedded in Western spatial systems. Ginnever's sculptures will always be different, for each viewer, each time they are seen. Years later Ratcliff described the ability of Chuck's work to reach beyond its own space, thus encouraging the eye to consider space itself as a flexible, inherently unstable medium in its own right.

Chuck has always brought certain concerns of his own—his mysteries of perception—to wide open sculptural environments. His works are of intense visual delight and they are decidedly peripatetic. Ginnever is quite skilled at playing against our visual habit—where the eye expects gravity to exert itself, the work springs into space, and as the spectator moves around it, a reading of material weight is challenged as the forms seem to disappear, as though suddenly weightless."

— Carter Ratcliff, summarized from Bruce Nixon
in Sculpture Magazine, Jan./Feb. 2004

"Charles Ginnever has been under-appreciated by critics, but he is an artist who has created a unique body of work that pulls us toward a visceral understanding of the nature of visual perception. Rooted in Japanese and Eastern teachings, Ginnever constructs large scale sculptures that must be experienced in situ. As the viewer moves around one of his elegant yet powerful metal constructions the landscape becomes the 'other element' in the work. A variety of vistas are framed while the form of the sculpture itself morphs Rashomon-like into different shapes—thereby underscoring the subjective nature of the way we see. Ginnever's multi-positional, interactive work plays against complacent visual tendencies, as the artist has noted, using traditional means to challenge atrophied habits of perception."

— Deborah Rothschild, Ph.D., Senior Curator Emerita,
Williams College Museum of Art, 2014